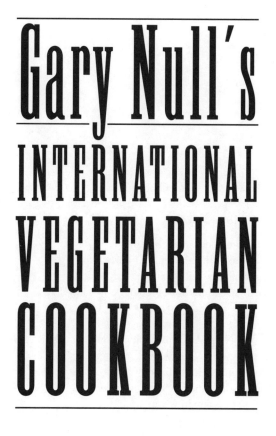

Gary Null's INTERNATIONAL VEGETARIAN COOKBOOK

BY GARY NULL

Macmillan • USA

D0038157

MACMILLAN
A Simon & Schuster Macmillan Company
1633 Broadway
New York, NY 10019

Macmillan Publishing books may be purchased for
business or sales promotional use. For information
please write Special Markets Department, Macmillan
Publishing USA, 1633 Broadway, New York, NY 10019.

Library of Congress Cataloging-in-Publication Data

Null, Gary
     Gary Null's International Vegetarian Cookbook/by Gary Null
       p.   cm.
     Includes index.
     ISBN 0-02-862327-4 (alk. paper)
     1. Vegetarian cookery. 2. Cookery, International. I. Title.
     TX837.N82   1998
     641.5'636—cd21   98-22861
                                    CIP

Manufactured in the United States of America
10 9 8 7 6 5 4 3 2 1

Book design by Amy Trombat

Contents

Introduction

WALK INTO ANY ALMOST BOOK STORE IN THE UNITED STATES AND YOU will find that the cookbook section is one of the largest and most popular. More Americans are interested in cooking—and in cooking for health—than ever before. Eighty-six million Baby Boomers are now at an age when they must pay attention to what they eat. They're beginning to see the causal relationship between good diet and good health, and they are battling excess weight as well. For good health and long life, many are ready to change the way they eat and cook.

But what kind of cooking to do? People eat junk food not only because it's convenient, but because they've acquired a taste for it after a lifetime of consuming it. To them it tastes good; vegetables don't. Statistics show that young Americans aged 2–18 have a disastrous diet, and most adults are not eating more than a single serving of fruit or vegetables a day. The challenge is to guide people who want to change their eating style but who want to do it with a sense of zest and excitement and with the goal of making healthy food more appealing than junk food.

The answer is to go global. When traveling to major cities in the United States, I've noticed that the least popular restaurants are those that serve American food. The far more enjoyable and commercially successful restaurants seem to be foreign: Chinese, Japanese, Spanish, Caribbean, French, Italian, Greek, Thai, Vietnamese. This book presents my favorite vegetarian dishes (some recipes incorporate fish, which many vegetarians do eat), from around the world. I have been testing these recipes for two years with people from my radio audience, starting with those listeners from the countries corresponding to the recipes, and then including others. I sought their feedback on taste, to ensure that each recipe would be one that cooks would return to again and again.

While taste was an important consideration, I knew I had to go further to create a superior cookbook by including foods with high nutritional value; foods with phytochemicals (the healing chemicals in plants); and ingredients low in sodium, fat, and cholesterol. I also placed a premium on ease of preparation, low expense, and minimal hassles in finding ingredients.

This book contains everything you will want to cook, so you can use it to plan entire meals: appetizers, soups, salads, side dishes, entrées, desserts, and sauces. Modify these recipes to suit your taste or that of your guests; cooking is a creative art. Improvise if you wish. The recipes make fewer servings than you usually see in cookbooks, for those readers who cook for themselves. I believe that cooking for one should be as delightful, rewarding, and healthful as cooking for many. It's easy to multiply the measurements for more servings.

Finally, I have tried to simplify things by keeping preparation time to a minimum. You do not have to be a gourmet chef to prepare these dishes, so enjoy!

Gary Null

Glossary of Ingredients

INGREDIENT	DESCRIPTION	SOURCE
Ackee	Tropical fruit used in Caribbean cuisine.	Caribbean market
Annatto seeds	Natural red-yellow food coloring.	Caribbean market
Arame	Sea vegetable, considered to have anti-cancer and immune enhancing components.	Oriental or healthfood market
Banana leaves	Used as a food wrapping in Caribbean baked dishes.	Caribbean market
Bragg's apple cider vinegar	Uncooked; less acidic than other vinegars.	Healthfood store
Bragg's liquid aminos	Source of protein from soy. May be used instead of tamari, soy sauce, or salt.	Healthfood store
Brown rice syrup	Sweetener made from brown rice.	Healthfood store
Calabaza	A West Indian pumpkin.	Caribbean market
Cassava	Starchy root used in bread and tapioca. Also known as as yucca among Latin Americans.	Caribbean or Latin American market
Chayote	A light green pear-shaped squash; also called *mirlitons*.	Latin American market
Date sugar	Natural, whole food sweetener made from dates.	Healthfood store
Dried bean curd cubes	Dehydrated tofu. Good in soups, as it will pick up the flavor of the liquid when reconstituted.	Healthfood store
Dulse	Sea vegetable used in soups and condiments. Considered to have anti-cancer and immune enhancing components.	Oriental market or healthfood store

Ingredient	Description	Source
Edible flowers	Violets, pansies, nasturtium, and others available in season. Used as garnish and in salads.	Specialty produce market
Egg substitute	Used in baking or as ingredient in cooking. Contains tapioca flour, potato starch, and leavening.	Health food store
Epazote	Pungent Mexican herb. Aroma and flavor when fresh much stronger than when dried.	Latin American grocery
Flaxseed	Used as thickener in cooking; also bulking agent in colon cleansing. Rich in immune-enhancing components.	Health food store
Garam masala	Blend of fragrant spices usually including cardamom, cinnamon, cloves, black pepper, and coriander.	Indian grocery
Garden Burger	Vegetarian burger made primarily of soy protein, wheat gluten, and spices. Non-soy version available for those allergic to soy.	Health food store
Garlic olive oil	Olive oil flavored with garlic.	Health food store
Jasmine basmati rice	Aromatic basmati rice from Thailand, with a nutty flavor.	Health food store or Indian market
Jicama	Potato-like root vegetable with a crunchy texture.	Mexican market
Kaffir lime leaves	Dried leaves of pear-shaped citrus fruit used in Southeast Asian cooking.	Asian market
Kombu	Mineral-rich sea vegetable. Considered to have anti-cancer and immune-enhancing components. Used especially in Japanese soup stock.	Health food store or Japanese market

Ingredient	Description	Source
Millet	High-protein, high fiber grain used in cereals and breads; alkalizing and antifungal.	Health food store
Miso paste	Paste made by the fermentation of soy or other beans and grains; rich in microorganisms that aid digestion. Used for flavor in oriental and macrobiotic cooking.	Oriental market or health food store
Mock chicken broth	Mix of soy, dehydrated vegetables, and spices.	Health food store
Morning Star Breakfast Links	Vegetarian sausage made primarily of soy.	Health food store
Name	A large, thick-skinned tuber with white, yellow or red flesh. Also called tropical yam.	Latin-American market
Nam prik paow	Oriental shrimp sauce.	Asian market
Nut Quick	Mineral-rich, almond-based beverage and baking mix.	Health food store
Plantain	Member of the banana family; higher in potassium. Must be cooked before eaten.	Latin-American market
Rice almond bread	Rich in nutrients; alternative for those allergic to wheat.	Health food store
Rice milk	Alternative to cow's milk; made from brown rice. Comes enriched and in a variety of flavors.	Health food store or supermarket
Rice stick noodles	Rice-based noodles used in Filipino cooking.	Oriental market
Safflower mayonnaise	Eggless, non-dairy, soy-based mayonnaise.	Health food store
Serrano chili	Variety of hot pepper; like jalapeño; used in Mexican cooking.	Gourmet or Latino food market

Ingredient	Description	Source
Shiitake mushrooms	Very flavorful variety of mushroom. Considered to be immune-enhancer, used as anti-cancer treatment.	Oriental market, gourmet store, or health food store
Soy cheeses	Available in Parmesan, cheddar, and mozzarella styles; solid, grated, and sliced.	Health food store
Soy mayonnaise	Eggless, non-dairy, soy-based mayonnaise.	Health food store
Soy milk	Alternative to cow's milk, made from ground soybeans and water. Comes in variety of flavors.	Health food store, supermarkets
Spelt bread	Higher-protein relative of wheat, without the allergenic properties.	Health food store
Stevia	Herb used widely in Japan as sweetener. Said to be 30 times sweeter than sugar. Virtually no calories; does not promote tooth decay.	Health food store
Succanat	Dehydrated pure juice of whole sugar cane.	Health food store, supermarket
Talapia	U.S. farm-raised fish	Fish market
Tamari	A milder soy sauce without wheat or artificial preservatives.	Health food store
Tamari roasted almonds	Almonds roasted in tamari; sold in bulk.	Health food store
Taro	Root vegetable used in Caribbean cooking. Dried leaves reconstituted in soups and stews.	Caribbean or Asian market
Tempeh	Made from unprocessed fermented soybeans. Contains B_{12} found only in animal products and live, fermented foods. Used as protein source by vegetarians.	Health food store

INGREDIENT	DESCRIPTION	SOURCE
Texturized vegetable protein (TVP)	Made from soy flour. Vegetarian replacement for ground meat in recipes such as chili and pasta sauce.	Health food store
Tofu	Vegetarian protein source; processed from soybeans. Good source of calcium and anti-cancer phytohormones.	Health food store, produce market
Tofu cream cheese	An excellent mimic, comes in vegetable and scallion varieties.	Health food store, bakery
Tomatillos	Small, green, tart fruit with papery husk.	Mexican market
Umeboshi plum paste	Japanese plum paste. Extremely salty; used for flavor in macrobiotic cooking; natural antibiotic.	Health food store, Oriental market
Ume vinegar	Vinegar made from umeboshi plums; much less acidic than most other vinegars.	Health food store, Japanese market
Veggie burger	Vegetarian burger made with combinations of vegetables, seeds, grains, and soy.	Health food store
Wakame	Sea vegetable, rich in calcium and niacin.	Health food store
Yellow bean sauce	Fermented beans made into sauce for dipping and cooking vegetables.	Chinese market
Yucca	Starchy root vegetable used in bread and tapioca. Also known as *cassava* among West Indians.	Latin American or Caribbean market

Chapter 1

APPETIZERS

Algerian
Cumin Flavored Chick Pea
Snack

Brazilian
Banana Farofa

English
Cucumber Queen

Indonesian
Seitan Coconut Fritters

Japanese
Japanese Fried Vegetables

Mexican
Virgin Sangria Drink

Puerto Rican
Fried Yuca

Vietnamese
Spring Rolls

Cumin Flavored Chick Pea Snack

yield 2 servings

12 ounces or 1 can chick peas	$1/8$ teaspoon freshly grated ginger
1 cup water	3 tablespoons lemon juice
3 tablespoons sesame oil	$1/4$ cup roasted pecans
$1/2$ cup finely chopped onion	4 tablespoons ground cumin
4 cloves garlic	1 teaspoon salt, or to taste
1 scallion, finely chopped	Radicchio, for garnish

1. Simmer chick peas in the water with sesame oil, onion, garlic, scallion, ginger, and lemon juice for 15–20 minutes until the chick peas are soft.

2. Add pecans, cumin, and salt; let cook 5 more minutes. Do not overcook or the mixture will become mushy. Drain.

3. Garnish with radicchio and serve.

Banana Farofa

yield 2 servings

3 bananas (half ripe), peeled
and cut into thick slices

3 tablespoons canola oil

1 medium vidalia onion, cut
into rings

2 tablespoons wheat germ

1. In a large skillet over medium heat, sauté bananas in canola oil until golden, then remove and set aside.

2. Using the same canola oil, sauté the onion rings.

3. Return the bananas to the pan with the onions, and gently stir in the wheat germ. Lightly brown the mixture on medium low heat. If it is noticeably dry, add more oil to loosen it. Serve hot.

Cucumber Queen

yield 2 servings

1 cucumber

1 small onion, cut into thin slices, about 1/4 cup

Pinch of salt

1 teaspoon rice wine vinegar

1/2 teaspoon honey

1 teaspoon fresh dill, chopped finely

Pinch of pepper

1 tablespoon minced green bell pepper

1 tablespoon alfalfa sprouts

Dash of paprika

1. Slice the cucumber in half lengthwise and scoop out the seeds. Slice the seeded cucumber crosswise into thin strips. In a bowl, combine it with the onion. Stir in remaining ingredients except sprouts and paprika.

2. Serve on toasted bread triangles or use as a filling for a sandwich. Top with alfalfa sprouts and dash of paprika.

Seitan Coconut Fritters

yield 2 servings

1 small hot chile pepper, diced

2 tablespoons lemon juice

1 teaspoon lime juice

2 tablespoons honey

1 teaspoon sea salt

Pinch cayenne

1 pound seitan

2 cups grated fresh coconut

Toasted peanut oil for frying

1. Blend chile, lemon juice, lime juice, honey, salt, and cayenne in a blender or food processor until a paste forms.

2. In a large bowl, thoroughly combine paste, seitan, and coconut.

3. In a deep skillet or wok, heat oil over moderate heat and fry fritters for 3–4 minutes.

4. Drain on paper towels and serve warm.

Japanese Fried Vegetables

yield 2 servings

SAUCE
1/4 cup sherry
1/2 cup tamari
Pinch grated fresh ginger

BATTER
1 cup spelt flour
1/2 cup ice water
1/8 teaspoon baking soda
2 tablespoons egg substitute

TO COMPLETE THE RECIPE
1/3 cup green beans
1 medium carrot, sliced very thin
1/2 cup broccoli flowerets
1/2 cup vidalia onion wedges
1 small zucchini
oil for frying

1. *To prepare the sauce*: Combine sherry, tamari, and ginger. Reserve for dipping the finished fried vegetables.

2. *To prepare the batter*: Mix spelt flour, ice water, baking soda, and egg substitute in a bowl. Use this batter for coating the vegetables.

3. *To complete the recipe*: Dip each piece of vegetable in the batter to coat, and fry in hot oil. Drain on paper towels. Serve with the dipping sauce.

Virgin Sangria Drink

yield 2 servings

1–2 jalapenõs, finely chopped
1/2 teaspoon fresh dill, finely chopped
1 cup tomato juice
1/4 cup lemon juice
1/2 cup orange juice
1/2 teaspoon paprika
1/2 teaspoon crushed coriander seed

1/2 teaspoon chili powder
1/8 teaspoon marjoram
1/8 teaspoon onion powder
1/8 teaspoon sea salt
1/8 teaspoon freshly ground black pepper
1/8 teaspoon crushed celery seed

Combine all ingredients and refrigerate 3–4 hours before serving.

Fried Yucca

yield 2 servings

2 small yucca (about ¹/₂ pound)

Vegetable oil for frying

1 teaspoon minced fresh parsley

¹/₂ teaspoon minced garlic

1 tablespoon olive oil

pepper to taste

1. Wash and peel yucca, and cut it into 2-inch × 1-inch pieces. Boil in salted water for 1 hour or until fork tender. Drain, and remove any fibrous pieces.

2. Heat 2 inches of oil to 350° in a heavy cast iron pot. Fry yucca, a few pieces at a time, until golden brown. Drain on paper towels.

3. Mix remaining ingredients and pour over yucca fritters before serving.

Spring Rolls

yield 2 servings

MARINADE

1 teaspoon egg white

$1/8$ teaspoon minced ginger

$1/4$ teaspoon minced garlic

$1/4$ teaspoon minced scallion

$1/2$ teaspoon tamari sauce

1 teaspoon dry sherry

FILLING

1 cup texturized vegetable protein (available in health food stores)

2 tablespoons mung bean sprouts, freshly rinsed

1 carrot, finely chopped

2 tablespoons finely chopped green cabbage

6 egg roll wraps

DIPPING SAUCE

$1/4$ cup fish sauce

1 tablespoon lime juice

1 tablespoon minced garlic

2 teaspoons honey

$1/2$ teaspoon minced jalapeño

$1/2$ teaspoon chile paste

2 teaspoons roasted chopped peanuts

1. *To prepare the marinade*: Combine marinade ingredients in a small bowl. Mix well.

2. *To prepare the filling*: Combine all filling ingredients except egg roll wraps in a separate bowl. Add the marinade, and mix well.

3. Follow directions on the egg roll wrap package to form spring rolls by rolling up the filling in the wraps.

4. *To prepare the sauce*: Combine ingredients for dipping sauce except peanuts in a separate bowl. Sprinkle chopped peanuts on top. Serve it in small bowls beside a plate of spring rolls.

Chapter 2

SOUPS

Algerian
Spicy Vegetable Pureé and
Swordfish Soup

Split Green Pea Soup

Bahamian
Conch Chowder

Belgian
Flemish Fish and Soup

Brazilian
Monkfish Soup and Rice

Burmese
Fish Soup

Chinese
Chinese Cabbage Soup

Oriental Cleansing Soup

Oriental Spinach and
Egg Drop Soup

Cuban
Vegetable Stew

Pureéd Plantain Soup

English
Mulligatawney Soup

French
Bouillabaisse (Fish Soup)

Onion Soup au Gratin

Two Potato Soup

Greek
Lemon Tree Soup

Hungarian
Potato Soup

Sauerkraut Soup

Spinach Soup

Queen's Soup

Indonesian
Egg and Ginger Ecstasy

Irish
Spring Stew

Fish 'n Chick Pea
Peppercorn Stock

Creamed Potato Soup

Italian
Rice and Bean Vegetable
Soup

Minestrone

Jamaican
Pureé with Rice

Pepperpot Soup

Pumpkin Soup

Vegetarian Root Soup

Mexican
Black Bean Soup

Polish
Borscht

Portuguese
Portuguese Kale-Potato Soup

Spanish
Gazpacho

Thai
Lemon Soup

Shrimp Hot and Spicy Soup

Turkish
Red Lentil Soup

Welsh
Leek-Potato Soup

Spicy Vegetable Purée and Swordfish Soup

yield 2 servings

1/2 tablespoon extra virgin olive oil

1 scallion, finely chopped

1 small onion minced, about 1/8 cup

1 clove garlic

1/2 pound swordfish steak, cut into 1-inch cubes

Pinch of salt

Pinch of black pepper

1/8 teaspoon sweet paprika

1 tablespoon cayenne

6 sprigs cilantro, trimmed, rinsed well, and tied with string

1/8 cup black-eyed peas, soaked overnight in water and drained

2 carrots, cut into 1-inch pieces

1 large potato, peeled and cubed

1 1/2 cups water

1 tablespoon tomato paste, dissolved in 2 tablespoons hot water

1 tablespoon (1/4 package) active dry yeast

1/8 cup whole wheat flour, dissolved in 1/8 cup warm water

1 1/2 teaspoons garam masala

Juice of 1/4 lime

1.   Heat the oil in a large pan. Add the scallion, onion, garlic, and swordfish, and stir-fry over moderate heat for 2 minutes. Add the salt, pepper, paprika, and cayenne and continue stirring.

2.   Add the cilantro, black-eyed peas, carrots, potatoes, and water and bring to a boil.

3. Add the tomato paste dissolved in water and continue to cook over moderate heat about 1 hour or until the swordfish is firm. Remove the swordfish and set aside. Remove and discard the cilantro.

4. While the soup is cooking, combine the yeast and flour-and-water mixture into a thick paste. Let it rise in a warm spot for 1 hour.

5. Pour the vegetables and broth into a blender and purée. Return the purée to the pan, add the swordfish, and simmer the soup over low heat. Stir in the garam masala, lime juice, and yeast-and-flour mixture. Simmer for 10 minutes to integrate all the flavors.

6. Serve warm with bread. You can also pass around a dish of lemon juice, which may be sprinkled to taste on the soup.

Split Green Pea Soup

yield 2 servings

2¹/2 cups water
¹/4 pound dried split green peas
1 large onion, chopped
2 scallions, chopped
2 cloves garlic, finely chopped
3 sprigs flat-leaf parsley, chopped

¹/2 teaspoon ground cumin
¹/4 teaspoon curry powder
¹/4 teaspoon pink or black French peppercorns
¹/4 teaspoon ground ginger
1 tablespoon olive oil
¹/2 teaspoon salt
Freshly ground black pepper

1.　Bring the water to a boil in a medium saucepan. Add the peas, and reduce the heat to low. Cook the peas for 1 hour or until the peas begin to disintegrate.

2.　Add the onion, scallion, garlic, parsley, cumin, curry powder, peppercorns, ginger, and olive oil and cook over low heat for ¹/2 hour. Add the salt and freshly ground pepper to taste.

Note *Should the soup become too thick, add water for desired consistency.*

Conch Chowder

yield 2 servings

1/2 pound fresh conch

3 cups water

Juice of 2 limes

2 tablespoons extra virgin olive oil

1 medium onion, chopped

2 stalks celery, minced

2 cloves garlic, minced

1 yellow pepper

2 scallions, whites only, chopped

1 tablespoon sherry

1 cup soy milk powder

1/2 cup diced carrot

1 large potato, peeled, boiled, and diced

1 bay leaf

1 small hot pepper (jalapeño is ideal)

1/4 teaspoon freshly ground black pepper

1 teaspoon sea salt

1/4 teaspoon dried thyme

1/2 teaspoon Pick a Pepper or Tabasco sauce

1 tablespoon mustard seeds

1 tablespoon fennel seeds

1 tablespoon honey

Parsley and Hungarian paprika for garnish

1. Simmer conch in 3 cups of water and lime juice for 30 minutes, then cool. Dice conch when cooled. Reserve cooking water.

2. In a stockpot, heat oil over medium heat and sauté onion, celery, garlic, yellow pepper, scallions, and sherry.

3. Using reserved water, reconstitute in blender 1 cup soy milk. Add to the sautéed vegetables the soy milk, diced conch, carrots, and potato. Add bay leaf, jalapenōs, pepper, salt, thyme, pepper sauce, mustard seeds, fennel seeds, and honey. Stir. Simmer an additional 15 minutes.

4. Garnish with parsley and Hungarian paprika.

Flemish Fish and Soup

yield 2 servings

FISH

1 pound perch, usually 1 medium fish

1 tablespoon olive oil

SOUP

1 quart water

1 cup white wine, Sauvignon Blanc or Chablis (regular cooking wine)

$1/2$ cup diced carrots

1 medium onion, chopped

1 teaspoon fresh chopped parsley

$1/4$ teaspoon dried tarragon

$1/4$ teaspoon crumbled sage

1 bay leaf

Dash of nutmeg

$1/4$ cup soy milk powder

$1/4$ cup water

Sea salt to taste

Freshly ground black pepper to taste

$1/2$ teaspoon caraway seeds

ORANGE GLAZE SAUCE

1 navel orange, peeled

2 tablespoons raw honey

1 teaspoon cooking sherry

$1/2$ teaspoon fennel powder

1 teaspoon pure vanilla flavor extract

Toasted pumpernickel rounds

1 tablespoon olive oil

1. *To prepare the fish*: Using a paper towel, lightly oil a broiling pan, then broil the fish on each side. Remove from oven and set aside.

2. *To prepare the soup*: Place the water, wine, carrots, onion, parsley, tarragon, sage, bay leaf, and nutmeg in a 2-quart soup pot. Bring the mixture to a boil, then lower the heat and simmer for 30 minutes.

3. Remove bay leaf from soup and blend mixture very briefly, allowing some texture to remain.

4. Add water to the soy milk powder until its consistency resembles heavy cream, then whisk the mixture into the soup pot and reheat on low. Add sea salt and pepper to taste.

5. Garnish soup with a sprinkle of caraway seeds, and serve alongside the broiled perch on a serving dish.

6. *To prepare the sauce*: Peel orange and put into a blender with the other sauce ingredients. Purée for 2 minutes or until a creamy consistency. Pour over fish.

7. Serve all with toasted pumpernickel rounds brushed with olive oil.

Monkfish Soup and Rice

yield 2 servings

1 pound monkfish fillet

2 tablespoons garlic or plain olive oil

1 cup Spanish onion, peeled and chopped

1/2 cup thinly sliced carrots

1 stalk celery, top included, chopped

3/4-inch piece fresh ginger, grated

1 fresh jalapeño, finely chopped

1/4 teaspoon annatto seeds

1 tablespoon powdered kelp

1/2 teaspoon celery salt

1/2 cup cubed hearts of palm

2 garlic cloves minced

1/2 cup fresh corn kernels off the cob, and 2 of the most tender husks

2 cups water

2 tablespoons canola oil

3/4 cup cooked brown basmati rice

1 tablespoon fresh cilantro leaves

2 tablespoons roasted pine nuts

1.   Place monkfish in a frying pan, and add enough water to cover plus 1/2 inch. Poach the monkfish just until done, so it flakes when tested with a fork. Drain and reserve the liquid. Cut the monkfish into cubes, cover, and refrigerate.

2.   In a sauté pan, heat olive oil, then add onion, carrots, celery, ginger, jalapeño, annatto seeds, kelp, celery salt, hearts of palm, and half of the minced garlic. Sauté, stirring, for 7 minutes.

3.   Purée corn husks in a blender with some water. Add purée to sauté pan.

4.   Transfer the contents of the sauté pan to a full-sized soup pot and add the reserved poaching liquid and 2 cups water. Simmer for 30 minutes.

5.   In a saucepan, heat the canola oil over medium heat and cook the remaining minced garlic for 3 minutes. Add brown rice and freshly cut corn, and stir in cilantro leaves. Cook over medium heat, stirring, 2-3 minutes.

6.   Combine rice-corn mixture with soup. Serve hot, sprinkled with roasted pine nuts.

Fish Soup

yield 2 servings

FISH BROTH

1 whole small white-fleshed fish (bass, haddock, flounder), about 1 pound, cubed

1 quart water

1 small onion, peeled and chopped

1 teaspoon sea salt

MARINADE

1 1/2 teaspoons tamari

1 tablespoon apple cider vinegar

Pinch of cayenne

TO COMPLETE THE RECIPE

1/8 cup long grain brown basmati rice

1/8 teaspoon crushed French or black peppercorns

1/2 cup shredded Chinese or green cabbage

1/4 cup slivered celery

1/4 cup honey

1. *To prepare the broth*: Trim off head, tail, skin, and bones from the fish and put trimmings in a kettle. Add water, onion, and sea salt. Bring to a boil. Cover and cook over low heat for 30 minutes. Strain the broth, discarding the solids.

2. *To prepare the marinade*: Mix tamari sauce, apple cider vinegar, and cayenne in a separate bowl. Allow the fish to marinate for 20 minutes.

3. *To complete the recipe*: Bring the broth to a boil again, add rice, and reduce heat to low. Cover and cook for 20 minutes.

4. Add fish cubes with peppercorns, cabbage, celery, and honey and continue cooking about 10 minutes, or until rice and fish are tender.

Chinese Cabbage Soup

yield 2 servings

SAUCE
1/2 teaspoon honey
2 teaspoons agar agar
1/8 teaspoon pepper
1 teaspoon tamari or shoyu
2 tablespoons sesame oil

TO COMPLETE THE RECIPE
2 ounces extra-firm tofu

1 teaspoon freshly grated
   ginger
1 clove garlic minced
1 teaspoon sea salt
2 cups shredded Chinese
   cabbage
3 cups water
1 tablespoon lemon zest

1. *To prepare the sauce:* Stir together honey, agar agar, pepper, tamari, and 1 1/2 tablespoons sesame oil.

2. *To complete the recipe:* Slice tofu horizontally in half then slice in ribbons. Cook tofu with sauce in a medium saucepan 5 minutes.

3. Place remaining 1/2 tablespoon oil in sauté pan over medium heat. Sauté ginger, garlic, and sea salt for 2 minutes. Transfer to a soup pot.

4. Add cabbage and 3 cups water. Cover and simmer for 10 minutes.

5. Add honey-tamari tofu sauce and simmer an additional 10 minutes.

6. Serve hot, sprinkled with lemon zest.

Oriental Cleansing Soup

yield 2 servings

1 cup vegetable broth

1/4 cup shredded greens (collard greens, kale, or beet greens)

1/4 cup dried bean curd cubes

1/8 cup bok choy leaves, thinly sliced

1/3 cup thinly sliced celery

1/2 cup water

1/4 cup egg substitute

1 tablespoon freshly squeezed lemon juice

1 grouper fillet

1. Place broth, greens, bean curd, bok choy, celery, and water in a pot. Slowly bring to a boil, then simmer for 30 minutes.

2. Slowly add egg substitute to simmering soup.

3. Sprinkle lemon juice over fish and drop the fish carefully into the pot. Continue to simmer for 6 minutes.

4. Serve immediately.

Note *This soup may be served with freshly chopped scallions on top. Or, take all the vegetables out after step 1 and eat as clear broth.*

Oriental Spinach and Egg Drop Soup

yield 2 servings

BROTH

1¹/2 cups water

¹/2 cup chickpeas, canned drained

OR

1 cup chick pea, vegetable, or mock chicken broth (all are available in health food stores; chick pea broth can be homemade, see step 1)

TO COMPLETE THE RECIPE

1 celery stalk

1 tablespoon chopped vidalia onion

¹/8 teaspoon lemon pepper

2 cups water

¹/2 cup shredded fresh spinach leaves, washed, drained, and patted dry

¹/2 cup egg substitute

1 teaspoon lemon juice

¹/3 cup fresh chopped scallion stalks

1.   *To prepare the broth:* Place ¹/2 cup chick peas in a large saucepan with 1¹/2 cups water. Cover and boil for 15 minutes.

2.   *To complete the recipe:* Add celery stalk, onion, lemon pepper, and 2 cups water to the broth. Bring to a boil and simmer for 1 hour. Discard the solid ingredients.

3.   Bring broth to a boil, add shredded spinach leaves, drop in egg substitute, and stir. Add lemon juice and garnish with chopped scallions. Serve immediately.

Vegetable Stew

yield 2 servings

1¹/2 cups lentils, rinsed

5 cups water

1 tablespoon olive oil

¹/2 yellow onion chopped

¹/2 green pepper chopped

2 minced garlic cloves

Pinch freshly ground black pepper

¹/4 teaspoon ground cumin

¹/4 cup crushed tomatoes (canned or fresh)

¹/2 medium yellow malanga (yam)

¹/2 medium white malanga (yam)

¹/4 medium name

¹/4 pound yucca

¹/4 pound calabaza (pumpkin)

Kernels shaved from one ear of corn

1 green plantain, cut in pieces

1 yellow plantain, cut into pieces

1 tablespoon lime juice

1. Place lentils and water in a stockpot, and boil for 15 minutes.

2. Meanwhile, heat oil in pan and sauté onion, green pepper, and garlic over medium heat until onions are translucent, about 2 minutes. Then add pepper, cumin, tomatoes, yellow and white malanga, name, yucca, calabaza, corn, green and yellow plantains, and more oil, if necessary, and sauté 2-3 minutes more.

3. Add vegetable mixture to boiling lentils.

4. Add the lime juice and simmer for 20 minutes.

Puréed Plantain Soup

yield 2 servings

One 16-oz. can chick peas
   with liquid
3 cups water
Pinch of white pepper
Pinch of salt

Pinch of cumin
1 cup salted plantain chips,
   ground in food processor
2 lime slices

1.   Combine chick peas, water, pepper, salt, and cumin in a large saucepan. Transfer 3/4 of the mixture to a blender or food processor and purée until smooth.

2.   Return the purée to the saucepan.

3.   Whisk ground plantain chips into the soup and heat.

4.   Garnish with lime slices.

Mulligatawny Soup

yield 2 servings

2 tablespoons walnut oil
1 small onion, chopped
1 scallion, chopped
1 clove garlic, chopped
1/2 cup apple, peeled, cored, and chopped
1/2 cup shredded carrot
1/2 cup chopped celery
1/4 cup coconut milk
1 teaspoon mild curry powder
1/4 teaspoon ground turmeric

1/4 teaspoon ground cumin
1 tablespoon chopped cilantro leaves
1 tablespoon chopped arugula
1 tablespoon rice flour
1 teaspoon arrowroot powder
3 cups vegetable broth or 3 cups water plus 2 vegetable bouillon cubes
1 Garden Burger (or other veggieburger) cut into cubes

1. In a large soup pot, heat the oil and cook the onion, scallion, garlic, apple, carrot, and celery for approximately 5 minutes.

2. Stir in the coconut milk and cook for 2 minutes. Add remaining ingredients except broth and Garden Burger and cook, stirring, an additional 3 minutes.

3. Slowly add the broth and bring to a boil. Cover, lower heat, and simmer for 15 minutes.

4. Place half the soup into a blender and purée. Return purée to the pot, and add the cubed Garden Burger. Cook an additional 3 minutes. Serve hot.

Bouillabaisse (Fish Soup)

yield 2 servings

1/8 cup sunflower oil

1 small leek, white part only, washed and chopped

3 shallots

3 cloves garlic minced

1 stalk celery chopped

1/8 teaspoon saffron

1 pinch crushed red pepper

1 bay leaf

1/4 teaspoon dried thyme

1/2 cup red wine, ideally Cabernet

31/2 cups fish or vegetable broth

11/2 cups crushed whole tomatoes (scalded, skinned, seeded, and chopped)

1/2 pound red snapper fillet, cubed

1/2 pound salmon fillet, cubed

1/2 pound grouper fillet, cubed

1/2 pound tuna fillet, cubed

Sea salt to taste

Freshly ground black pepper to taste

1.   Heat oil in a saucepan over medium-high heat. Sauté leek, shallots, garlic, and celery until soft, about 5 minutes.

2.   Stir in saffron, crushed red pepper, bay leaf, thyme, wine, and broth. Bring to a boil and then simmer uncovered 30 minutes.

3.   Discard bay leaf. Purée crushed tomatoes and leek mixture in a blender or food processor. Return to saucepan and bring to a simmer.

4.   Add fish and continue simmering gently about 5 minutes. Add salt and pepper to taste.

Onion Soup au Gratin

yield 4 servings

1¹/2 tablespoons olive oil

1 large onion, thinly sliced

Sea salt to taste

Freshly ground black pepper to taste

¹/8 teaspoon honey

1 tablespoon spelt flour

Bouquet garni of 10 parsley sprigs, ¹/4 teaspoon thyme, 3 peppercorns, and 1 bay leaf tied into a cheesecloth sack

2¹/2 cups vegetable broth

¹/2 cup Bragg's Liquid Aminos (available at health food stores)

¹/4 cup white wine, ideally Chablis

4 slices seven-grain bread, cut into 1 inch thick rounds

1 tablespoon almond oil (divided)

1 small clove garlic, minced

¹/2 cup grated soy or nut cheese

1. Heat the oil in a large covered saucepan. Cook the onions with a pinch of salt and pepper in the saucepan over medium-low heat, stirring occasionally, until soft.

2. Add honey, and continue cooking uncovered over medium heat, stirring occasionally, until the onions are golden brown.

3. Add the flour and cook, stirring constantly, for 3 minutes. Add the bouquet garni, broth, liquid aminos, wine, a dash more salt and pepper, and cook for 30 minutes partially covered, skimming occasionally.

4. Preheat oven to 350°. Arrange the bread on a baking sheet. Brush both sides with half of the almond oil and minced garlic. Lightly toast in the oven, turning once, until golden-brown.

5. Remove the bouquet garni and pour the soup into four oven-proof bowls. Cover the top of each bowl with toast. Sprinkle the toast with cheese and drizzle with the remaining almond oil.

6. Bake the soup 15-20 minutes, or until simmering. Place under the broiler for 2 minutes, or until cheese is golden. Serve immediately.

Two Potato Soup

yield 2 servings

1 tablespoon canola oil

2 leeks, white part only, sliced

1/8 cup minced shallots

1 small vidalia onion, chopped

2 large baking potatoes, peeled and diced

1 medium sweet potato, peeled and diced

2 cups water or clear vegetable broth

1 tablespoon orange blossom honey

1/8 teaspoon cayenne

1 dried chile, crushed

1/2 cup soy or rice milk

Sea salt to taste

Freshly ground black pepper to taste

1/8 cup chopped chives

1. Heat the oil in a heavy saucepan over medium heat. Cook leeks, shallots, and onion until very soft, approximately 8 minutes.

2. Add potatoes and cook 2 minutes. Stir in broth and honey, bring to a boil, and reduce heat. Simmer about 20 minutes, or until potatoes are tender.

3. Purée soup in a blender until very smooth. Return purée to pot, add cayenne, chile, and soy milk, and reheat on low, stirring constantly with a wire whisk.

4. Season with sea salt and pepper to taste. Serve garnished with chives.

Lemon Tree Soup

yield 2 servings

CELERY BROTH
1 cup celery broth

TO COMPLETE THE RECIPE
2 cups chick pea broth (see page 23) or mock chicken broth (available at health food stores)

1 tablespoon ground flaxseed or arrowroot
^{1}/2 cup basmati rice
^{3}/4 cup egg substitute
Sea salt to taste
Freshly ground black pepper to taste
Juice of 2 large lemons

1. *To prepare broth*: Simmer 6 sliced celery stalks in 1^1/4 cups water for 15 minutes. Discard celery.

2. *To complete the recipe*: Put celery broth and chick pea broth in a large saucepan and slowly bring to a boil. Add ground flaxseed.

3. Stir in rice, cover, and reduce heat. Simmer 10-15 minutes until rice is tender.

4. In small bowl, beat egg substitute until creamy. Season with salt and pepper. Add lemon juice and 2 ladles of broth. Add mixture slowly to broth, stirring constantly. Beat until light and creamy. If soup is too thin, add more ground flaxseed.

5. Over low heat, stir slowly until soup thickens. Make sure soup does not boil. Serve at once.

Note *This soup does not reheat well.*

Potato Soup

yield 2 servings

2 medium potatoes, peeled and cubed

1 carrot, diced

1 stalk celery, chopped

4 cups boiling water

1 onion, finely chopped

1 1/2 tablespoons walnut oil

3 Morning Star Breakfast Links, or other vegetarian sausage, cut into small pieces

1 tablespoon tapioca

3 tablespoons honey

1/2 cup reconstituted dry soy milk, made extra thick

Sea salt to taste

Freshly ground pepper to taste

1 cup toast cubes

1.　In a large saucepan, combine the potatoes, carrot, and celery. Cover with boiling water and cook until tender.

2.　In a sauté pan, brown the onion in the oil over medium high heat. Add the vegetable sausage pieces, and cook until browned.

3.　In a large bowl, combine tapioca, honey, and reconstituted soy milk to make a cream mixture.

4.　Pour the hot soup over the cream mixture and mix thoroughly. Season with salt and pepper to taste.

5.　Pour into warm soup bowls. Top with toast cubes.

Sauerkraut Soup

yield 2 servings

1 cup prepared sauerkraut

2 cups water

1¹/2 tablespoons avocado or olive oil

1 small onion, finely chopped

¹/4 teaspoon paprika

3 Morning Star Breakfast links or other vegetarian sausage, sliced thin

1¹/2 tablespoons soy flour

MOCK SOUR CREAM

¹/4 package silken tofu

1 teaspoon freshly squeezed lemon juice

1.   Boil the sauerkraut in the water until tender.

2.   In a large pan, heat the oil and sauté the chopped onion over medium-low heat. Add the paprika.

3.   Brown the vegetarian sausage links with the onion. Remove one sausage link and set aside.

4.   Stir the soy flour into the sausage/onion mixture. Thin by whisking ¹/2 cup of the sauerkraut liquid into the mixture. Add the remaining sauerkraut and cook for 5-7 minutes.

5.   *To prepare the sour cream:* In a blender, purée the tofu and lemon juice to the consistency of sour cream.

6.   Ladle the soup into bowls. Top each bowl with a dollop of the mock sour cream. Garnish each serving with one slice of the sausage link previously set aside.

Spinach Soup

yield 2 servings

1/2 pound spinach, well washed, with stems removed (1 pound fresh equals 1/2 pound after stems removed)

2 cups water

1/4 teaspoon sea salt

1 medium onion, finely chopped

1 tablespoon olive oil

2 tablespoons whole wheat flour

1/2 cup reconstituted soy milk powder, extra thick to resemble cream

1 hard boiled organic egg, sliced

Edible flowers for garnish

1. In a medium pot, simmer the spinach in salted water until soft. Strain the spinach and reserve the liquid. Rub the spinach through a strainer or purée in a blender.

2. In a large saucepan, brown the onions in the oil. Slowly blend in the flour.

3. Add 1/2 cup of the spinach liquid and cook, stirring with a wire whisk, until thick and smooth. Add the remaining liquid and the spinach. Heat to boiling.

4. Remove from heat and blend in the thickened soy milk. Garnish with egg slices and colorful flowers.

Queen's Soup

yield 2 servings

1 cup chick peas

2 cups water

1 quart water

1 tablespoon hazelnut or olive oil

1/4 cup yellow onion, finely minced

1/4 teaspoon saffron

Pinch of dried peppermint leaves

1 tablespoon tamari

1/8 cup white Jasmine basmati rice

Mock Sour Cream (see page 33)

1. Soak chick peas overnight in 2 cups water. Discard liquid, and then simmer chick peas in 1 quart water for 1 1/2 hours until soft. Strain and reserve broth. Refrigerate chick peas for garnish and another use.

2. In a saucepan, heat oil and sauté onion. Add chick pea broth, saffron, mint, and tamari. Add rice and simmer. When rice is tender, put through a food mill.

3. Serve hot, with a dollop of Mock Sour Cream and some chick peas and a crouton on top.

Egg and Ginger Ecstasy

yield 2 servings

1/4 cup firm tofu, finely cubed

1 teaspoon cayenne

1/4 teaspoon cumin

Freshly ground black pepper to taste

1 tablespoon fat free Caesar salad dressing

1 small onion, peeled and chopped

3/4 tablespoon olive oil

1/3 cup chick pea broth (see page 23)

3 cups vegetable broth, fresh or prepared

1 teaspoon freshly grated ginger

1 tablespoon fresh-squeezed lemon juice

1-2 elephant garlic cloves or 4 regular cloves, crushed

1/2 cup celery, thinly sliced

1/3 cup fresh scallions, chopped

3/4 cup egg substitute

1.   Soak tofu cubes in 1/8 teaspoon cayenne, 1/8 teaspoon cumin, black pepper, and Caesar salad dressing for 15 minutes.

2.   Sauté onion, 1/8 teaspoon cayenne, and 1/8 teaspoon cumin in olive oil over medium heat until tender. Set aside in a warm place.

3.   In a large saucepan, place chick pea broth, vegetable broth, the remaining cayenne, ginger, lemon juice, garlic, and celery. Bring to a boil. Lower heat and simmer, covered, for 10 minutes.

4.   Remove tofu cubes from dressing and drain.

5.   Divide half the scallions and the egg substitute between 2 hot bowls. Fill the bowls with broth, add tofu cubes, and sprinkle the top with onion mixture and more scallions.

Spring Stew

y i e l d   2   s e r v i n g s

6 medium baby red potatoes

2 large vidalia onions, thinly sliced, divided into thirds

1/2 teaspoon cumin

1/2 teaspoon fresh Italian parsley

Sea salt

Black pepper

1 sprig of fresh dill

1 sprig of fresh thyme

2 cups water

1/4 cup dried beans (chick peas or red beans) soaked overnight

Two 8-ounce tuna steaks

1.   Peel all potatoes and thinly slice a third of them; leave the rest whole.

2.   Place a layer of thinly sliced potatoes in an ovenproof saucepan, then add one-third of the onions. Sprinkle with cumin, parsley, and salt and pepper to taste. Add dill, thyme, and another third of sliced onion. Cover with the whole potatoes. Correct seasonings.

3.   Add 2 cups of water and the beans, and cover the pot with a tight-fitting lid. Bake in the oven for 2 hours at 350° (or you may simmer gently on the stovetop for the same time). The thinly sliced potatoes on the bottom will thicken the juice.

4.   Add tuna steaks and the remaining onions, and cook for 15-25 minutes longer. Serve hot in big bowls.

Fish'n Chick Pea Peppercorn Stock

yield 2 servings

1 salmon fillet (swordfish or blackfin shark may be substituted)

2 cups chick pea broth (see page 23)

1/8 teaspoon finely ground ginger

1/2 cup canned vegetable broth (or use mix found in health food stores)

2 vidalia onions, chopped

6 cloves

6 peppercorns

2 cups cold water

1/4 teaspoon cumin

1/4 teaspoon thyme

Pinch fresh oregano

1 bay leaf

1 tablespoon Italian parsley, freshly chopped

1/4 cup celery, thinly sliced

1/2 teaspoon soy sauce

4 carrots

1/4 cup shredded red cabbage

1. Put all the ingredients in a medium to large pot and boil for 2 hours. (You may need to add water during cooking.) Strain through a fine sieve, being careful to capture all solids so they do not go into the broth. Discard all but the broth.

2. Store broth in a glass jar in the refrigerator for up to 4 days for making another soup or sauce. May also be used in small amounts for additional flavor in recipes calling for water.

Creamed Potato Soup

yield 2 servings

1 large russet potato, peeled
  and cubed

2 tablespoons canola oil

1 small leek, chopped

2 scallions, chopped

1/2 onion, chopped

1/2 teaspoon sea salt

2 tablespoons rice flour

1/2 cup powdered soy milk

2 cloves garlic, chopped

1/2 cup watercress, finely
  chopped

1 teaspoon cumin

1 teaspoon cayenne

Sprinkle of Cajun spices

1. Boil potato in at least 2 1/4 cups salted water. Drain, reserving 2 cups of the potato water. (Add more water if you need to.)

2. Heat canola oil in pan, and sauté leek, scallions, onion, and salt for 10 minutes. Sprinkle flour over mixture, and stir to coat.

3. Combine 1/2 cup powdered soy milk with 1/2 cup potato water; stir until smooth. Stir soy milk into leek mixture.

4. In blender, purée garlic and potato with the remaining 1 1/2 cups potato water. Return puréed potatoes to original boiling pan, and whisk in the leek mixture. Add 1/4 cup watercress, cumin, and cayenne. Reheat for 5 minutes.

5. Garnish with remaining watercress and Cajun spices.

Rice and Bean Vegetable Soup

yield 2 servings

1¹/2 tablespoons extra virgin olive oil

1 onion, finely chopped (use vidalia for milder taste)

1 tablespoon fresh parsley, chopped

1/2 clove elephant garlic, peeled and crushed, or 3 regular cloves

1/3 tablespoon dried thyme

1 tablespoon tomato paste

2 cups water

1/2 teaspoon cumin

1/2 cup chopped celery

4 sprigs saffron

1 tablespoon oregano

1/4 teaspoon dried basil

1/4 teaspoon cayenne

1/4 cup corn, or kernels from 1 ear

2 large tomatoes, peeled, seeded, and chopped

1/2 cup shredded red cabbage

1 zucchini, diced

1 carrot, diced

1/4 cup fresh green peas

1/2 quart vegetable broth

Salt to taste

Freshly ground black pepper to taste

1/2 cup cooked rice

2/3 cup cooked or canned white or yellow beans

1/2 cup grated Parmesan or Romano cheese, or soy substitute

2 tablespoons fresh minced parsley

1. Heat olive oil in a 3-quart saucepan and gently cook the onions, parsley, garlic, and thyme until the onions are soft.

2. Thin the tomato paste with ¹/8 cup water, add to saucepan, and cook for about 4 minutes.

3. Add cumin, celery, saffron, oregano, basil, cayenne, corn, tomatoes, cabbage, zucchini, carrot, green peas, and vegetable broth. Season with salt and pepper to taste. Simmer covered for about 30 minutes, or until the vegetables are tender.

4. Add the rice and beans and cook until heated through, about 3 minutes. If desired, add extra water.

5. Mix the grated cheese with the parsley and sprinkle over each bowl before serving.

Minestrone

yield 2 servings

3 tablespoons olive oil

1 onion, peeled and chopped

3 cloves garlic, chopped

1/2 cup red cabbage, minced

1 cup extra firm tofu, cut into 1/4-inch cubes

2 stalks celery, diced

1/2 tomato, peeled, seeded, and chopped

2 medium carrots, diced

1 potato, peeled and diced

1/2 cup fresh basil

5 bay leaves

1/2 tablespoon dill

1/2 tablespoon fennel

1 cup tomato sauce

1/4 cup water

1/2 cup cooked white beans

1/2 teaspoon sea salt

1/4 teaspoon red pepper

1/2 cup dried pasta shells

1/8 cup soy parmesan cheese

1.   In a stockpot, heat the olive oil over medium heat and sauté the onion, garlic, and cabbage with the tofu until the onion is soft.

2.   Add the celery, tomato, carrots, potato, basil, bay leaves, dill, and fennel. Mix well to combine.

3.   Add the tomato sauce and water, bring to a boil, and simmer for 10 minutes.

4.   Stir in the beans, salt, pepper, and pasta. Cook for about 8 minutes or until done.

5.   Serve hot topped with soy parmesan cheese.

Purée with Rice

yield 2 servings

1 pound callaloo leaves, bok choy or Swiss chard, finely chopped

1 scallion, finely diced

2 garlic cloves, finely diced

12 small okra pods, trimmed and chopped

2 sprigs of parsley, chopped

1 stalk of celery, with leaves, chopped

1/4 teaspoon dried thyme

2 tomatoes, cored and chopped

1 bay leaf

1 tablespoon avocado or canola oil

Sea salt to taste

Freshly ground black pepper to taste

Dash of cayenne

1/2 cup vegetable broth or water

1 cup cooked white basmati rice

1. Put all the ingredients except the rice in a large saucepan. Cover with water or broth and simmer, covered, for 1 hour.

2. Blend the soup with a wire whisk.

3. Serve hot with a scoop of rice in the center.

Pepperpot Soup

yield 2 servings

1 pound kale or collard
greens

3/4 pound callalo or bok choy

1 small onion, chopped

1 small yam, peeled and
diced

6 fresh okra pods, cut into
small rings

1/2 pound taro root, peeled
and diced

2 cloves garlic, minced

2 large scallions, finely
chopped

1 sprig thyme, leaves only

1/2 teaspoon ground ginger

Pinch of paprika

1 jalapeño or habañero pepper (about 1/4 teaspoon)

1 tablespoon avocado or
canola oil

2 cups bacon-flavored tofu
crumbles

1 cup coconut milk

1. Steam all greens and vegetables in a large covered soup pot
until soft. Rub all ingredients through course strainer, colander, or
food mill and return to soup pot.

2. Add all seasonings, peppers, avocado oil, and tofu crumbles.
Add coconut milk and heat through on medium-high, about 5 minutes. Serve hot.

Pumpkin Soup

yield 2 servings

1 medium onion, chopped

1 tablespoon olive oil

2 tablespoons golden miso

1 pound pumpkin (or calabaza or Hubbard squash), diced

2 scallions, with tops, chopped

3 cloves garlic, crushed

1 Scotch Bonnet pepper

1 sprig fresh thyme

1 yellow pepper, stemmed and seeded

1 marjoram sprig (or $^1/4$ teaspoon dried)

1 bay leaf

1 teaspoon tamari

Pinch of nutmeg

Dash of hot pepper or Tabasco sauce

Sea salt to taste

White pepper to taste

Fresh parsley for garnish

1.   In a large soup pot, sauté onion in oil over medium heat until translucent.

2.   Add remaining ingredients except parsley and cover with water. Simmer until pumpkin is tender.

3.   Garnish with dried parsley. Serve with toasted black Russian bread.

Vegetarian Root Soup

yield 2 servings

2 tablespoons avocado or
olive oil

1/2 cup Bermuda onion,
chopped

1 cup okra, sliced

1 1/2 cups celery, diced

1/2 cup chayote, peeled and
diced

1 cup fresh mushrooms,
sliced

2 cloves garlic, minced

1/4 cup wakame leaves

1 cup potato, peeled and
diced

1/2 cup calabaza or pumpkin
or butternut squash,
peeled and diced

1 teaspoon fresh chile,
seeded and minced

1 cup tomato juice

2 tablespoons fresh squeezed
lime juice

1/2 cup presoaked pigeon
peas

1 tablespoon sago or
2 tablespoons arrowroot

1 teaspoon cilantro, chopped

Dash of nutmeg

1/4 teaspoon allspice

Pinch saffron

1/2 teaspoon sea salt

1 slice lime and parsley for
garnish

1. In a large soup pot, heat oil over medium heat and sauté onion, okra, celery, chayote, mushrooms, garlic, and wakame for 30 minutes.

2. Add potato, calabaza, chile, tomato juice, lime juice, peas, and cover with 1/2-inch of water.

3. Mix sago or arrowroot with enough water to make a smooth sauce, then add to soup pot with a whisk.

4. Add cilantro, nutmeg, allspice, saffron, and sea salt. Cover and cook over medium heat until vegetables are soft.

5. Garnish with lime and parsley, and serve with no-salt crackers.

Black Bean Soup

yield 2 servings

1/4 cup olive oil

2 cloves garlic, minced

1 1/2 onions, chopped

1/2 teaspoon grated orange rind

1/2 teaspoon sea salt

1/2 teaspoon freshly ground black pepper

1/2 teaspoon honey

1/2 teaspoon fennel seed

1/2 teaspoon celery seed

1/2 teaspoon dried basil

1/2 teaspoon dry mustard

1/4 teaspoon allspice

1/2 cup firm tofu, cubed

1 cup canned black beans

Optional seasonings to taste: paprika, chili powder, black pepper, garlic powder, onion powder, celery seed, basil, marjoram, oregano, cayenne

3/4 cup tomato sauce

3 tablespoons freshly squeezed lemon juice

1. Heat oil in a medium saucepan over medium heat, and sauté garlic, onions, and all seasonings.

2. Add tofu and beans, cover, and simmer 15-20 minutes. Use additional seasonings to taste.

3. Add tomato sauce and lemon juice and serve hot.

Borscht

2 cups fresh beets, peeled and chopped

5 cups water

1 tablespoon lemon juice

4 tablespoons lime juice

1/4 cup whole wheat flour

3 tablespoons olive oil

2 yellow onions, diced

2 cups small red potatoes, diced

1 bunch lemongrass, diced

2 tablespoons parsley, finely chopped

3 tablespoons mint, minced

Mock Sour Cream (page 33)

1.   In a medium saucepan, simmer the beets in the water, lemon juice, and lime juice for 1/2 hour.

2.   Add the flour, olive oil, onions, and potatoes and simmer for 10 minutes, stirring continuously.

3.   Season with lemongrass, parsley, and mint. Serve hot, garnished with a dollop of Mock Sour Cream.

Portuguese Kale-Potato Soup

yield 2 servings

1/2 pound fresh kale or Swiss
  chard
1 medium potato, peeled
4 cups water
1/8 cup full-bodied extra
  virgin olive oil

Sea salt to taste
Freshly ground black pepper
  to taste
Pinch of nutmeg
3 teaspoons spearmint leaves

1. Wash kale and cut off stems. Twist leaves tightly in a circular fashion and slice into very thin shreds. Set aside.

2. In a large soup pot, place potato, water, oil, salt, and pepper and bring to a boil. Reduce heat to a simmer. Cover and cook slowly about 25 minutes, or until potato is tender.

3. Purée soup in food processor or blender. Return purée to soup pot and add kale strips, nutmeg, and spearmint. Cook about 15 minutes more or until kale is tender. Serve hot.

Gazpacho

yield 2 servings

1 yellow pepper

1 red pepper

1/2 cucumber

3 ripe medium tomatoes, peeled and seeded

1 small onion

2 cloves garlic, crushed

1 tablespoon balsamic vinegar

1/4 cup olive oil

2 cups cold water

Sea salt to taste

1/4 teaspoon crushed red pepper

1/4 pound tempeh

Finely chopped onion, pepper, and cucumber for garnish

1. Dice the peppers, cucumber, tomatoes, onion, and garlic, then combine them in a bowl with vinegar, oil, water, salt, and crushed red pepper. In a blender or food processor, purée mixture until smooth. Refrigerate for 2 hours.

2. Slice tempeh into chunks, and pour purée over tempeh. Garnish each serving with onion, pepper, and cucumber.

Lemon Soup

yield 2 servings

1¹/2 cups light fish broth (see below), or mock chicken or vegetable broth

1 teaspoon avocado or olive oil

1 carrot, chopped

1 stalk celery

1 small onion, chopped

1 thick stalk lemongrass, finely chopped

1¹/2 tablespoons freshly squeezed lemonjuice

¹/2 teaspoon freshly squeezed lime juice

2 Kaffir lime leaves, chopped

¹/2 fresh red chile pepper, thinly sliced

¹/2 teaspoon lemon zest

³/4 teaspoon date sugar or raw brown sugar

Lemon pepper or black pepper to taste

1 teaspoon chopped cilantro leaves

¹/2 cup croutons

1. *To prepare fish broth:* In a medium saucepan, simmer 4 oz. of any white-fleshed fish in 1³/4 cup of water for 20 minutes. As an alternative, 1¹/2 cups of vegetarian mock chicken or vegetable broth (available in health food stores) may be used.

2. In a wok, heat oil, stir in the broth, carrot, celery, and onion. Bring to a boil, then reduce heat and simmer for 20 minutes. Strain broth and return liquid to wok. Discard vegetables.

3. Add lemongrass, lemon juice, lime juice, lime leaves, chile, lemon zest ,and date sugar. Add lemon pepper or black pepper to taste.

4. Serve hot, garnished with floating cilantro and croutons.

Shrimp Hot and Spicy Soup

yield 2 servings

2 vegetable bouillon cubes in 2 cups boiling water

2 teaspoons **nam prik paow** (shrimp sauce)

1 stalk lemongrass

2 fresh Kaffir lime leaves, center vein removed

1-2-inch piece fresh ginger

1/2 cup shiitake mushrooms, sliced

1/4 cup green cabbage, shredded

1 scallion, chopped

1 carrot, shredded

2 teaspoons shoyu sauce

1/2 teaspoon cayenne

1 teaspoon dry sherry

1/2 pound shrimp, preferably prawns, shelled and deveined

1 tablespoon lemon juice, divided

1 teaspoon minced fresh coriander leaves for garnish

1.   In a medium saucepan over high heat, bring to a boil the vegetable broth, *nam prik paow,* lemongrass, lime leaves, ginger, mushrooms, cabbage, scallion, carrot, shoyu, cayenne, sherry, and half of the lemon juice. Reduce heat to low and simmer, covered, 10 minutes.

2.   Bring mixture back to a boil. Drop in prawns and cook 2 minutes. Stir in the remaining lemon juice and coriander. Serve hot.

Red Lentil Soup

yield 2 servings

1/2 cup red lentils	Pinch of saffron threads
1/4 cup walnut oil	1 tablespoon fresh mint, chopped
1/2 cup chopped onion	1 teaspoon fennel seeds, crushed
2 cloves garlic, minced	1 teaspoon fresh parsley, chopped
2 vegetable bouillon cubes	2 slices of toasted spelt or rice bread (available in health food stores)
4 cups water	
1 1/2 tablespoons spelt flour	
1/4 cup egg substitute	
1/2 cup plain soy milk	

1. Cover lentils with water and soak overnight in closed container. Drain and discard water.

2. In a soup pot, heat 1/2 tablespoon of the walnut oil over medium-high heat, and lightly brown the onions and garlic. Add bouillon cubes, water, and lentils. Bring to a boil.

3. Slightly reduce heat and cook, covered, for 30 minutes or until lentils are quite soft. Remove from heat, and keep covered.

4. In a small saucepan, create a sauce by melting together the remaining walnut oil with spelt flour and egg substitute. Stir carefully for 2 minutes. Gradually add 1/2 cup of lentil mixture, stirring constantly until sauce thickens.

5. Process the remaining lentil mixture in a blender until consistency is uniform. Return mixture to the large soup pot.

6. Add sauce and soy milk to pot. Add saffron, and simmer for 10 minutes.

7. Top with mint, fennel seeds, parsley, and broken bread toasted until crouton-like.

Leek-Potato Soup

yield 2 servings

2 leeks, white parts and tops	1 bay leaf
1¹/2 cups soy or rice milk	¹/8 teaspoon dried thyme
2 tablespoons soy or spelt flour	1 sprig parsley
Canola oil	Sea salt to taste
1 tablespoon sunflower oil	Freshly ground black pepper to taste
2 medium potatoes, peeled and sliced	¹/2 tablespoon chopped chives for garnish
1 cup water	

1. Thinly slice tops of leeks. Dip them in milk as a wash, then dust with flour. Reserve the remaining milk.

2. Pour 1¹/2 inches of canola oil in a small saucepan. Heat the oil to medium and fry the leek tops until golden-brown. Drain on paper towels and set aside.

3. Wash the white parts of the leeks and slice into coin-shaped pieces. Sauté in heated sunflower oil in a large saucepan until tender.

4. To the large saucepan add potatoes, water, bay leaf, thyme, parsley, sea salt, and pepper. Bring to a boil. Reduce heat and cook slowly, covered, until potatoes are tender, approximately 25 minutes.

5. Remove from heat and discard bay leaf and parsley.

6. Purée the mixture in a blender, and return to saucepan over medium-low heat. Slowly add remaining soy milk. Heat through gently, stirring frequently, being careful not to let the mixture boil.

7. Garnish with chopped chives and the leek tops and serve.

Chapter 3

SALADS

African American

Potato Salads I & II

Algerian

Autumn Salad

French

Endive Salad

German

Cucumber Salad

Hot Potato Salad

Greek

Grecian Olive and
Rice Salad

Italian

Insalata Siciliana

Mexican

Zesty No Dish Avocado

Polish

Herbed Tomato Salad

Orange, Cabbage, and
Leek Salad

Thai

Thai-style Salad

Turkish

Chilly Cucumber and Tofu

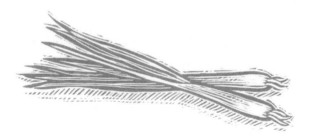

Potato Salads I & II

yield 2 servings

1/2 pound red potatoes	1/2 cup soy mayonnaise (available at health food stores)
1 medium celery stalk, minced	
1/2 small onion, minced	Sea salt to taste
1 tablespoon parsley, minced	Freshly ground pepper to taste
1 tablespoon dill, minced	

1. Wash potatoes and steam until tender but not mushy, about 20 minutes. Drain, peel, and allow to cool.

2. Place celery and onion in a large bowl. Add parsley and dill.

3. When potatoes have cooled, cut them into 1/2-inch dice and add them to the onions and celery.

4. Add the mayonnaise a little bit at a time until the mixture is well coated, but not too wet. Add salt and pepper to taste and mix well. Cover with plastic wrap and refrigerate. Serve chilled.

VARIATION

Add 1/8 cup each minced red and green bell pepper, 1 hard-boiled egg coarsely chopped, and 2 tablespoons sweet pickle relish.

Autumn Salad

yield 2 servings

SALAD

2 large Honeywell oranges
(or oranges in season)

1/2 grapefruit

1 medium bunch watercress

1 1/2 large handfuls radicchio

1 handful red leaf lettuce

1/4 bulb fennel

1 carrot, shredded

1/4 cup Bermuda onion,
thinly sliced

1 scallion, chopped

1/4 cup pitted green or black
olives

VINAIGRETTE

3 tablespoons extra-virgin
olive oil

2 teaspoons balsamic vinegar

1 teaspoon capers, smashed

1 teaspoon apple cider
vinegar

1 teaspoon red wine vinegar

1/4 teaspoon sea salt

Freshly ground black pepper
to taste

1. *To prepare the salad:* Slice off both ends of oranges and grapefruit. Standing each fruit on end, carefully cut away the peel and skin to expose the fruit. Cut each fruit in half lengthwise twice to form four wedges.

2. Wash and dry watercress, radicchio, and red leaf lettuce, removing any tough stems.

3. Remove the core from the fennel, then shave the bulb thinly along the grain.

4. *To prepare the vinaigrette:* Combine ingredients in a small bowl and stir briskly.

5. To present salad, arrange oranges, grapefruit, fennel, carrot, onion, scallion, and olives in center of platter. Cover with half the vinaigrette. In a bowl, lightly toss the greens with the rest of the vinaigrette, and distribute the greens around the arrangement.

Endive Salad

yield 2 servings

1/4 pound endive
1/4 pound Granny Smith
   apples
1 cup small mushrooms
1/3 cup tofu cream cheese
   (see Note below)

1/4 cup hazelnuts, chopped
Pinch of sea salt
Freshly ground black pepper
1/4 cup cooked beets,
   chopped
Fresh lemon juice

1.   Trim endive and cut leaves into thick slices.

2.   Peel and core apples and cut into small chunks.

3.   Slice mushrooms.

4.   Place endive, apples, and mushrooms in a salad bowl.

5.   In a separate bowl, combine tofu cream cheese with hazelnuts and salt and pepper to taste. Pour mixture over salad vegetables
and toss together.

6.   Sprinkle beets over salad, then sprinkle with lemon juice to
taste.

Note   *To prepare tofu cream cheese, blend tofu with rice milk to form
a liquid the consistency of heavy cream.*

Cucumber Salad

yield 2 servings

1 large cucumber

1 tablespoon onion, diced

1 tablespoon fresh green pepper, diced

1 tablespoon fresh red pepper, diced

1 tablespoon scallion, chopped

$1/2$ teaspoon prepared stone ground mustard

$1/2$ teaspoon apple cider vinegar

1 tablespoon plain soy milk

$1 1/2$ teaspoon canola oil

Sea salt to taste

Freshly ground pepper to taste

1. Peel cucumber and cut in half. Remove seeds, and cut into very thin slices. Combine in a bowl with onion, peppers, and scallion.

2. In a small bowl, stir together mustard, vinegar, and soy milk. Pour over cucumber mixture, add canola oil, and mix well. Season to taste with sea salt and pepper.

Hot Potato Salad

yield 2 servings

3 large potatoes or 7 baby new potatoes

1 tablespoon white or yellow onion, diced

1 tablespoon dulse leaves, chopped

1 tablespoon extra-virgin olive oil, plus extra for sautéing

1^1/2 tablespoon Braggs liquid aminos (available at health food stores)

^{1}/3 cup hot water

1 garlic-pickle or cucumber, diced

1 tablespoon ground fennel seed

^{1}/2 teaspoon lemon juice

2 sprigs fresh parsley, chopped

Sea salt

Freshly ground pepper

1. Boil potatoes in their skins until tender. Discard skins and slice potatoes in a large bowl.

2. Sauté onion and dulse in a few drops of oil over medium high heat.

3. Mix aminos with water and pour over cooked potatoes.

4. Add the onion, dulse, pickle, and fennel. Mix well. Add 1 tablespoon olive oil and sprinkle with lemon juice and parsley. Add small amount of water if dry. Serve hot, adding salt and pepper to taste.

Grecian Olive and Rice Salad

yield 2 servings

3/4 cup uncooked basmati rice

1 cup distilled water

3/4 teaspoon fresh oregano, finely chopped (or 1/2 teaspoon dried)

1/8 cup Italian parsley, finely chopped

1 3/4 tablespoons extra-virgin olive oil

1 tablespoon balsamic vinegar

1/2 clove garlic, pressed

1 tablespoon hazelnuts, finely chopped

Sea salt to taste

Freshly ground black pepper to taste

5 or 6 Greek olives, green and black, pitted and chopped

4 cups (about 6 oz) spinach leaves, washed, dried, and steamed until just wilted

1/4 cup crumbled tempeh

Parsley for garnish

1.   Cook rice according to package directions.

2.   In glass jar, mix water, oregano, parsley, olive oil, vinegar, garlic, hazelnuts, salt, and pepper. Cover tightly and shake well.

3.   Combine rice and chopped olives in a bowl. Pour dressing over mixture and toss.

4.   Arrange steamed spinach leaves on 2 plates, fill with rice and olive mixture and sprinkle tempeh on top. Garnish with parsley.

Insalata Siciliana

yield 2 servings

$^1/_2$ cup broccoli flowerets

$^1/_2$ cup arugula, chopped

$^1/_2$ cup cherry tomatoes, chopped

$^1/_2$ red pepper, diced

$^1/_2$ yellow pepper, diced

$^1/_4$ cup artichoke hearts, chopped

$^1/_2$ pound mushrooms, sliced

$^1/_4$ cup gherkins, sliced

8 green and black pitted olives

$^1/_2$ cup peas

$^1/_2$ teaspoon fresh oregano

1$^1/_2$ tablespoons capers

1 cup canned cannelloni beans

Sea salt to taste

Freshly ground black pepper to taste

$^1/_2$ teaspoon lemon juice

$^1/_4$ cup extra-virgin olive oil

$^1/_8$ cup balsamic vinegar

1. Toss broccoli, arugula, tomatoes, peppers, artichoke hearts, mushrooms, gherkins, olives, peas, oregano, capers, and beans in a salad bowl. Season with salt and pepper.

2. Add lemon juice, oil, and balsamic vinegar and toss lightly.

Zesty No Dish Avocado

yield 2 servings

1 large avocado, sliced in half
  lengthwise and pitted

1 serrano chile with seeds,
  diced

3/4 cup fresh cilantro leaves,
  diced

2 tablespoons freshly
  squeezed lime juice

1 teaspoon sea salt

1 pound tomatillos, husked
  and chopped

Pinch freshly ground cumin

Parsley for garnish

Slices of red and green bell
  pepper for garnish

1. With a spoon, scoop out all avocado flesh; reserve the skins. Place the flesh with all other ingredients except garnishes in a food processor and purée.

2. Fill the avocado skins with the purée. Garnish with parsley and bell pepper slices. Chill in refrigerator for 1 hour, then serve.

Herbed Tomato Salad

yield 2 servings

1 teaspoon sea salt

$^1/_2$ teaspoon freshly ground
black pepper

$^1/_8$ teaspoon cayenne

2 tablespoons lime juice

2 tablespoons fresh dill

$^1/_2$ tablespoon chopped fresh
thyme

3 ripe tomatoes

1 bunch arugula

1 bunch watercress

1.   Combine salt, pepper, cayenne, lime juice, dill, and thyme.

2.   Cut tomatoes into thick slices; toss with arugula and watercress. Pour dressing over salad, and let salad marinate for 1 hour in
refrigerator. Serve chilled.

Orange, Cabbage, and Leek Salad

yield 2 servings

3 cups red cabbage, shredded

3 oranges, peeled and seg-
mented

1/4 cup olive oil

4 tablespoons lime juice

2 tablespoons lemon juice

6 tablespoons honey

2 tablespoons mint, minced

4 tablespoons fresh basil,
minced

Orange segments and edible
flowers (if available) for
garnish

1. In a large bowl, toss together cabbage and oranges.

2. In a separate bowl, combine oil, lime juice, lemon juice,
honey, mint, and basil. Mix together salad and dressing, and marinate
in refrigerator for 1 hour before serving.

3. Garnish the plate with a flower and fanned orange segments
and serve chilled.

Thai-style Salad

yield 2 servings

1 cup bean threads

1/4 cup onion, grated

1/4 cup cucumber, thinly sliced

4 ounces firm tofu, sliced into thin, 2-inch strips

1 stalk lemongrass, thinly sliced

1/8 cup fresh lime juice

1 teaspoon rice vinegar

1 tablespoon fish sauce

2 red chile peppers, seeded and chopped

8 mint leaves

2 scallions, tops included, chopped

1/2 cup cooked chick peas

1 tablespoon fresh parsley, chopped

1 teaspoon honey

1/8 teaspoon allspice

1 small Boston lettuce

radish slices for garnish

1.   Cover bean threads in warm water and soak for 15 minutes. Drain and slice into 3-inch strips.

2.   In a salad bowl, combine bean threads, onion, cucumber, tofu, lemongrass, lime juice, rice vinegar, fish sauce, red chiles, mint leaves, scallions, chick peas, parsley, honey, and allspice.

3.   Line salad bowl with Boston lettuce leaves, and spoon salad mixture into center. Garnish with radish slices.

Chilly Cucumber and Tofu

yield 2 servings

1 small cucumber

1 teaspoon sea salt

1 dash Mrs. Dash Table Blend

1 clove garlic, cut in half

1 cup silken tofu

1 teaspoon freshly squeezed lemon juice

2 teaspoons apple cider vinegar

1^1/2 teaspoons Spectrum's Mediterranean Oil or olive oil

^{1}/8 cup fresh dill, chopped

^{1}/8 cup fresh mint, chopped

^{1}/4 teaspoon jalapeño or Tabasco sauce

Dash of paprika

1. Peel cucumber and slice lengthwise. Remove seeds by running a spoon down entire inside length. Grate cucumber coarsely, collecting the juice and pulp in a bowl. Sprinkle with sea salt and Mrs. Dash. Set aside.

2. Prepare another bowl by rubbing the inside with the two garlic halves.

3. In a blender, blend the garlic halves, tofu, lemon juice, vinegar, Mediterranean oil, half of the dill, half of the mint, and the pepper sauce.

4. Pour cucumber pulp and tofu mixture into garlic-rubbed bowl. Chill thoroughly.

5. Serve garnished with a pinch of reserved dill and mint and dash of paprika.

Chapter 4

SIDE DISHES

Algerian
Spinach Sauté
Tuna-Egg Balls

Cuban
Red Beans with Rice

French
Braised Endive

German
Bavarian Cabbage

Greek
Stuffed Grape Leaves
Mediterranean Garlic Tahini
Eggplant

Guyanaian
Roti Bread

Hungarian
Galuska
Potato Dumplings

Indian
Spiced Potatoes

Irish
Irish Soda Bread with
Caraway

Italian
Red Tomato Pilaf

Jamaican
Bammie Cakes
Jamaican Seasoned Rice

Mexican
Yellow Rice

Polish
Mushroom Stuffed Tomatoes
Potato Pancakes

Portuguese

Portuguese Corn Bread

Spanish

Pisto

Roasted Peppers with
Vinaigrette

Saffron Rice

Thai

Golden Rice

Yellow Bean Eggplant

Turkish

Positively Pea Pilaf

Bread Hoops

Spinach Sauté

1/2 pound fresh spinach, well
  rinsed, drained, and
  stemmed

1 1/2 tablespoons peanut oil

1/2 cup chopped Spanish or
  yellow onion

2 cloves garlic, crushed in a
  garlic press

1/2 teaspoon anchovy paste

1 cup tomatoes, skinned and
  chopped

1/4 cup black olives, sliced

1/4 teaspoon white pepper

1. Steam the spinach in 1/4 cup water until wilted. Discard cooking liquid or save for another recipe. Shake or press out any liquid. Set spinach aside.

2. Heat peanut oil in a nonstick skillet over high heat. Stir fry onion, garlic, and anchovy paste.

3. Add tomatoes, olives, and pepper.

4. Add spinach and stir. Cover, reduce heat to low, and cook for 10 minutes.

Tuna-Egg Balls

yield 6 balls

$^1/_2$ pound fresh cooked or canned tuna

$^1/_2$ small onion, chopped (about $^1/_4$ cup)

$^1/_2$ teaspoon sea salt, or to taste

$^1/_8$ teaspoon freshly ground black pepper

$^1/_8$ teaspoon ground cinnamon

$^1/_8$ teaspoon cayenne

$^1/_4$ teaspoon dried mustard

1 scallion, chopped

$^1/_2$ teaspoon diced fresh red pepper

$^1/_2$ teaspoon Braggs liquid aminos (available at health food stores)

2 tablespoons egg substitute

$^1/_2$ cup spelt flour

3 hard-cooked organic eggs

3 tablespoons olive oil

Lemon wedges

1. Flake tuna and mix with onion, salt, pepper, cinnamon, cayenne, dried mustard, scallion, red pepper, aminos, and egg substitute. Combine into a smooth paste. Add flour until the mixture thickens. Set aside.

2. Peel eggs, then cut them in half crosswise. Take about 2 heaping tablespoons of the tuna mixture and cover each egg half. Wrap the tuna mixture around the egg to make a ball.

3. Heat olive oil in a wok or skillet over moderate heat and fry balls 3 or 4 minutes to brown. Drain briefly on paper towels.

4. Serve warm with lemon wedges.

Cuban

Red Beans with Rice

yield 2 servings

1/2 medium yellow onion, chopped

2 cloves garlic, peeled and mashed

1/2 green bell pepper, chopped

1 tablespoon olive oil

1 cup cooked red kidney beans

2 cups water

1 tablespoon honey

3/4 cup short grain brown rice

1 tablespoon tamari sauce

Pinch fresh ground pepper

Pinch cumin

1/2 teaspoon sea salt

Colorful edible flowers or parsley for garnish

1.   Sauté onion, garlic, and pepper in oil until golden. Place the sautéed ingredients into a saucepan, along with all remaining ingredients except the flowers or parsley.

2.   Simmer until rice is al dente or to taste, about 35 minutes.

3.   Garnish with colorful flowers or parsley and serve.

Braised Endive

3 endives

1/2 tablespoon walnut oil

1/2 tablespoon peanut oil

Sea salt

Freshly ground black pepper

1/2 teaspoon date sugar or 2 tablespoons maple syrup

1/2 tablespoon fresh lemon juice

1/2 teaspoon lime juice

1 teaspoon Braggs liquid aminos (available at health food stores)

1 tablespoon water

1/2 tablespoon chopped parsley

1. Preheat oven to 350°.

2. Trim and core the endives. Moisten a paper towel with vegetable oils and oil the bottom and sides of an ovenproof dish. Put the whole endives in the dish.

3. Sprinkle endives with sea salt, pepper, date sugar, lemon and lime juices, liquid aminos, and 1 tablespoon water.

4. Cover with aluminum foil and bake until endives are tender inside, approximately 50 minutes. Garnish with chopped parsley.

Bavarian Cabbage

yield 2 servings

1 small onion, diced

1 clove garlic, chopped

1 ounce kombu or arame seaweed, soaked in water for about 20 minutes to reconstitute

2 tablespoons olive oil

$^1/_4$ teaspoon date sugar or 2 tablespoons maple syrup or honey

$^1/_2$ pound green cabbage, shredded

$^1/_4$ pound red cabbage, shredded

1 Granny Smith apple, diced

$^1/_4$ cup white wine (Chardonnay is ideal)

$^1/_4$ cup water

Sea salt

1 tablespoon white wine vinegar

1. In a large pan over medium heat, sauté onion, garlic, and seaweed in oil until onions are golden.

2. Stir in sugar and add cabbages and apples. Mix well, cover, and cook over low heat approximately 30 minutes.

3. Add wine and water. Cover and cook approximately 20 minutes more. Season with salt and vinegar.

Stuffed Grape Leaves

yield 20 grape leaves

FILLING

1/2 yellow onion, chopped
1 clove garlic, chopped
1 carrot, chopped
1 tablespoon olive oil
1 cup tomato juice
1 cup shiitake mushrooms
1/2 cup cooked brown rice
1/4 cup corn kernels

1 teaspoon curry powder
Sea salt to taste
Freshly ground black pepper
   to taste

TO COMPLETE THE RECIPE

20 grape leaves washed thoroughly
1 lemon

1. Preheat oven to 300°.

2. *To prepare the filling:* Over medium heat, sauté chopped onion, garlic, and carrot in oil until browned. In a large bowl, mix well with tomato juice, mushrooms, rice, corn, curry powder, salt, and pepper.

3. *To complete the recipe:* Place a grape leaf, shiny side down, on a board. Place 1 teaspoon of filling in center of grape leaf. Form into a roll, making sure shiny side of leaf is on the outside. Repeat with remaining leaves and filling.

4. Pack rolls firmly in baking dish, squeeze lemon on top, and add enough water to cover.

5. Bake 1/2 hour. Serve hot.

Mediterranean Garlic Tahini Eggplant

yield 2 servings

1 large eggplant ($1^1/_2$-$1^3/_4$ pounds)

4 cups ice cold water

3 tablespoons freshly squeezed lemon juice

$^1/_4$ teaspoon hot Hungarian paprika (use less for milder flavor)

$^1/_4$ teaspoon cayenne

4 teaspoons tahini

2-3 tablespoons fresh garlic, chopped

$^1/_8$ teaspoon dried thyme

1 tablespoon extra-virgin olive oil

$^1/_2$ teaspoon sea salt

Freshly ground black pepper to taste

Red and green bell peppers, sliced

Vine ripe tomatoes, diced

$^1/_2$ tablespoon fresh parsley, chopped

1. Preheat oven to 375°.

2. Using a toothpick or fork, pierce the eggplant several times, and place in an oiled baking dish. Bake until tender, about 50 minutes.

3. Place eggplant in large pot of ice cold water to cool quickly. Remove peel while steam is still present. Drain in colander until eggplant cools completely. Squeeze pulp to remove any bitter juices, and then purée the flesh.

4. In a large bowl, mix together lemon juice, paprika, cayenne, tahini, garlic, and thyme. Adjust quantities for spicy or mild preferences. Purée in food processor. If necessary, thin with water, or thicken with $^1/_8$-$^1/_3$ teaspoon flaxseed.

5. While processor is running, add eggplant, olive oil, salt, and pepper to taste.

6. Spread the mixture in a shallow serving dish, and garnish with sliced red and green bell peppers, tomatoes, and parsley.

Roti Bread

yield 2 servings

ROTI

1/2 cup whole wheat pastry
   flour
1/2 cup rice or soy flour
1 teaspoon baking powder
1/2 teaspoon sea salt
Rice milk, chilled
Peanut oil

TOPPING

1 small onion, diced
1 large clove garlic, thinly
   sliced
1 tablespoon curry powder
1 teaspoon dried dill
1 cup seitan
2 teaspoons peanut oil

1.   *To prepare the roti:* Sift dry ingredients into a bowl. Add just enough rice milk to make a stiff dough. Form 4 small balls.

2.   Roll out into 6-inch circles. Brush lightly all over with oil, then sprinkle with flour. Fold in half, then in half again, forming a 4-layered quarter circle. Cover and let stand for 30 minutes.

3.   Heat griddle or iron skillet with small amount of peanut oil. Unfold each roti back into a circle and heat in pan for 1 minute. Then drizzle top of roti with hot oil and turn. Cook each side until golden brown.

4.   Remove from pan to a board. Hit with either a wooden mallet or palm of hands, clapping hands until the bread is flaky.

5.   *To prepare the topping:* In a medium skillet, sauté onion, garlic, curry powder, dill, and seitan in peanut oil until onion is translucent, about 5 minutes.

6.   Serve roti hot with topping, or with vegetable curry and chutney.

Galuska

yield 2 servings

SOFT NOODLES

1 cup spelt flour
$1/3$ cup water
2 tablespoons egg substitute
$1/2$ teaspoon sea salt
$1/2$ teaspoon olive oil

SAUCE

2 fresh tomatoes, cubed
$1/2$ bell pepper, chopped
$1/2$ red pepper, chopped
$1/2$ onion, chopped

1.   *To prepare the noodles:* Put the flour in a large bowl and make a well in the center. Add water, egg substitute, salt, and olive oil to the well. Mix everything lightly until well blended.

2.   Put a portion of the dough on a small, wet bread board. Flatten the dough. Using a wet knife, cut the dough into 1 × 3-inch pieces.

3.   Push dough pieces off the board into boiling salted water. They are done when they rise to the top. Skim noodles off and pile in a hot dish.

4.   *To prepare the sauce*: Sauté tomatoes, peppers, and onion for about 15 minutes. Serve over noodles.

Potato Dumplings

yield 2 servings

1 medium-large potato,
  cooked and peeled

2 teaspoons olive oil

$1/4$ teaspoon sea salt

$1/4$ cup egg substitute

1 cup dried bread cubes,
  about $1^1/2$ slices of bread

2 teaspoons walnut oil

$1/4$ teaspoon white pepper

$1/4$ teaspoon garlic powder or
  1 clove garlic, minced

Arugula and tomato wedges
  as garnish

1. Over a large bowl, mash potato through a strainer.

2. In another bowl, combine the olive oil, sea salt, and egg substitute. Mix into the potatoes.

3. Lightly brown the bread cubes in the walnut oil, adding pepper and garlic while stirring gently with a fork. Press the bread cubes into the potato mixture.

4. Shape into small dumplings and cook in gently boiling salted water about 15 minutes. Avoid overcooking.

5. Serve on a bed of arugula and garnish with tomato wedges.

Spiced Potatoes

yield 2 servings

1 pound russet potatoes

2 tablespoons hazelnut oil

1 teaspoon cumin

1 small ripe tomato, peeled and chopped, about 1/4 cup

1/2 teaspoon cayenne

1/2 teaspoon turmeric

1 tablespoon barley malt syrup

1 tablespoon soy yogurt

1/2 teaspoon ground fresh ginger

1/2 tablespoon ground cloves

1/2 tablespoon dried tarragon

1/2 tablespoon fresh basil, chopped

Freshly ground black pepper to taste

1 teaspoon sea salt

1/4 cup water

1. Boil whole potatoes, skins on, until almost soft. Remove, cool, and peel. Set aside.

2. Heat the oil in a pan over moderate heat. Brown whole potatoes on all sides, about 3 minutes. Remove potatoes and set aside. Discard all but 1 tablespoon oil.

3. Heat the tablespoon of oil over moderate heat and stir-fry cumin for 10 seconds.

4. Add tomato, cayenne, turmeric, and barley malt syrup and stir-fry for 2 minutes.

5. Add soy yogurt, ginger, cloves, tarragon, basil, and pepper. Stir for 3 minutes.

6. Add whole potatoes, salt, and water and simmer, covered, over low heat until water evaporates and a thick sauce remains.

Irish Soda Bread with Caraway

yield 2 servings

1 1/2 cup sifted rice flour
1/4 cup sifted buckwheat flour
1/4 cup sifted oat flour
1/3 cup honey plus additional to brush on bread
2 cups vanilla soy milk
1 teaspoon baking soda or baking powder

1/2 teaspoon sea salt
1 tablespoon caraway seeds
1/2 teaspoon vanilla extract
Handful of raisins
Olive oil to grease the pan (olive oil cooking spray preferred)

1. Preheat oven to 350°.

2. In a bowl, mix all ingredients except oil. Stir well to combine, and then turn the mixture into an oiled mixing bowl.

3. Lightly flour hands, and blend ingredients until a firm, ball-shaped dough forms. Place into an oiled metal baking pan. Dust a knife with flour and make an X on top of the loaf.

4. Bake 45-60 minutes. Do not allow top to brown. About 5 minutes before bread is done, use a pastry brush to brush the top with honey, if desired. Serve at room temperature.

Red Tomato Pilaf

yield 2 servings

2 tablespoons extra-virgin olive oil

1 small onion, diced

1 clove garlic, minced

2 small or 1 large tomato (approximately 8 ounces), chopped

2 tablespoons fresh parsley, chopped

1 1/2 tablespoons fresh basil chopped

1/4 teaspoon dried marjoram

3/4 cup cooked white basmati rice

1 1/4 cups vegetable broth

Pinch saffron

Pinch cayenne

Sea salt to taste

1.   In a saucepan, heat the oil over moderate heat, and sauté onion and garlic, covered, for about 3 minutes, or until onion is translucent.

2.   Add tomatoes, parsley, basil, and marjoram, and sauté 5 minutes.

3.   Add rice, vegetable broth, saffron, cayenne, and sea salt. Bring to a boil, then reduce to a simmer. Cover and cook for 5 minutes.

4.   Remove from heat. Remove lid, and cover with a cloth towel to allow evaporation of excess water vapor without loss of heat. Let stand 10 minutes. Serve alone or as a vegetable stuffing.

Bammie Cakes

yield 2 servings

1 pound cassava

1 tablespoon olive oil

1/4 cup vidalia onion, chopped

1 teaspoon Cajun seasoning

1/4 teaspoon sea salt

1/8 teaspoon freshly ground black pepper

1 tablespoon egg substitute mixed with 1 tablespoon water

3 tablespoons honey

1/4 cup chopped walnuts

Olive oil for frying

Red cabbage, shredded, for garnish

1. Peel cassava and grate it finely with grater or in food processor. Using cheesecloth, strain out as much juice as possible. (Raw cassava juice is not safe to cook with or to drink.)

2. In a large pan, heat olive oil over medium heat and sauté onion with Cajun seasoning, salt, and pepper.

3. In a bowl, combine egg substitute mixture and honey.

4. Add cassava flour and stir in onion and walnuts.

5. In a heavy skillet, heat 1/4 inch of oil on medium-high. On a sheet of wax paper, mold the cassava pancakes and then transfer into skillet. Fry until both sides are toasty crisp. Serve warm, garnished with shredded cabbage.

Jamaican Seasoned Rice

yield 2 servings

3/4 pound brown short grain basmati rice

1 large carrot, peeled and sliced

1 small chayote

1 1/2 cups pumpkin, canned or fresh

1/3 pound broad beans, soaked overnight

1 sweet red pepper, chopped

1 sweet potato, peeled and diced

2 scallions including tops, chopped

1 large ripe tomato, cored and chopped

2 tablespoons canola margarine

1/4 teaspoon dried thyme

Hot pepper sauce (such as Tabasco) to taste

Sea salt to taste

Olive oil

Romaine lettuce for garnish

1. Steam rice until just tender.

2. In a large pot, place carrot, chayote, pumpkin, beans, sweet pepper, sweet potato, scallions, and tomato. Cover with water and cook over medium heat until tender. Drain liquid.

3. Add margarine, thyme, Tabasco sauce, salt, and rice.

4. In a large nonstick pan, heat a small amount of olive oil. Transfer the rice mixture into the pan. Cook on medium-low heat for 10 minutes to marry the flavors.

5. Garnish with romaine lettuce, and serve hot.

Yellow Rice

yield 2 servings

1 cup short grain brown rice

1/2 red onion, sliced

4 serrano chiles, stemmed and sliced

1 teaspoon sea salt

3 cloves garlic, crushed

4 tablespoons olive oil

11/2 cups water

11/2 teaspoons ground annatto seeds

1/2 tomato, peeled and chopped

1/4 cup peas

1/2 cup red and yellow peppers, diced

1/2 teaspoon dried epazote

Seasonings to taste: sea salt, paprika, chili powder, black pepper, garlic powder, onion powder, celery seed, basil, marjoram, oregano, cayenne.

1.   In a pan over medium heat, sauté rice, onion, chiles, salt, and garlic in oil 3-5 minutes.

2.   Place the water and annatto seeds in a medium saucepan, and bring to a boil. Add the rice and return to a boil.

3.   Reduce heat, stir in tomato, peas, peppers, epazote, and a pinch of each of the seasonings. Cover and simmer 15-20 minutes or until rice is done and liquid is evaporated.

Mushroom Stuffed Tomatoes

yield 2 servings

2 large tomatoes

1/2 pound fresh white
mushrooms, sliced

2 tablespoons olive oil

1/2 cup bread crumbs

1 teaspoon sea salt

1/4 teaspoon white pepper

1 tablespoon toasted sesame
seeds

1 tablespoon dried basil

1. Preheat oven to 350°.

2. Slice tops off tomatoes, and set aside. Scoop out tomato seeds.

3. In a pan over medium heat, sauté mushrooms in olive oil 5-10 minutes, then combine with bread crumbs, salt, pepper, sesame seeds, and basil.

4. Fill tomatoes with mushroom stuffing. Cover with tomato tops, and place in a shallow, greased pan. Bake 25-30 minutes, and serve warm.

Potato Pancakes

yield 2 servings

3 new potatoes, peeled $1/4$ cup egg substitute
$1/2$ cup rice milk $1/4$ teaspoon cinnamon
$1/8$ teaspoon sea salt   2 tablespoons canola oil

1. Boil potatoes until tender, and then mash them.

2. Add milk, salt, and egg substitute to mashed potatoes, and sprinkle in the cinnamon.

3. Shape into individual cakes and sauté in medium-hot oil until golden brown.

Portuguese Corn Bread

yield 2 servings

1/2 teaspoon sea salt
1 cup yellow cornmeal
1 1/2 cups spelt flour
2 teaspoons rapid rise yeast
1/2 cup fresh or frozen corn,
    slightly crushed

1 teaspoon honey
1/2 cup water
1/2 cup rice or soy milk
1 1/2 teaspoons corn oil

1.   Combine salt, cornmeal, spelt flour, and yeast in a deep bowl. Add the corn.

2.   Place honey, water, milk, and corn oil in a pan and heat to 110-113°, or until it feels slightly warm to your wrist. (You can use a candy thermometer to check the temperature.)

3.   Mix the dry ingredients with the wet ingredients and shape into a round ball. If dough is too sticky, add more flour. Place dough into a greased soufflé pan. Place in a warm spot away from drafts, and allow to rise until doubled in bulk, approximately 1-1 1/2 hours.

4.   Preheat oven to 350°.

5.   After bread has risen once, bake in the same pan 30 minutes or until loaf sounds hollow when tapped.

Pisto

yield 2 servings

1 large yellow onion, chopped

2 bell peppers, green and red, chopped

2 cloves garlic, chopped

1/4 cup olive oil

1/2 large eggplant, diced

1 zucchini, diced

2 large ripe tomatoes, peeled and chopped

Seasonings to taste: sea salt, paprika, chili powder, black pepper, garlic powder, onion powder, celery seed, dried basil, dried marjoram, dried oregano, cayenne

1. In a large saucepan, sauté the onion, peppers, and garlic in the oil until soft.

2. Add eggplant, zucchini, tomatoes, and desired seasoning, and stir well. Cover and cook over medium heat 30-40 minutes.

3. Remove from heat. Let stand a few minutes before serving.

Roasted Peppers with Vinaigrette

yield 2 servings

2 large bell peppers, red and
yellow

1/2 tablespoon wine vinegar

2 teaspoons olive oil, plus
additional to oil baking
sheet

Sea salt to taste

Freshly ground black pepper
to taste

1 artichoke heart, quartered

3 hearts of palm

1.   Preheat oven to 350°.

2.   Bake whole peppers on an oiled baking sheet 25-30 minutes,
turning every 10 minutes. Remove from oven.

3.   In a small bowl, combine vinegar, olive oil, salt, and pepper,
and set aside.

4.   When peppers are cool, peel them and cut them in half.
Discard the seeds and cut peppers into strips. Mix with artichoke
heart and hearts of palm. Pour vinaigrette over vegetables before
serving.

Saffron Rice

yield 2 servings

$1/2$ sweet red pepper, sliced thinly

$1/2$ sweet yellow pepper, sliced thinly

1 medium onion, chopped

2 cloves garlic, minced

2 tablespoons olive oil

2 cups basmati rice

3 cups boiling water

Pinch of saffron

1 teaspoon sea salt

$1/2$ cup cooked peas

1. In a saucepan, sauté peppers, onion, and garlic in the oil until soft.

2. Add rice and stir until grains are coated with oil. Add water, saffron, and salt.

3. Cover and simmer for approximately 20 minutes until rice is cooked and all the water is absorbed. Add peas and fluff with a fork. Serve warm.

Golden Rice

yield 2 servings

1³/4 cups boiling water
1 teaspoon sea salt
1 cup uncooked brown jas-
    mine basmati rice
1 clove garlic, minced
1 scallion, chopped
1 tablespoon onion, minced
2 tablespoons olive oil

³/4 cup (6 ounces) coconut
    milk
2 curry leaves or bay leaves
¹/4 teaspoon ginger powder
¹/2 teaspoon turmeric
1 teaspoon parsley, minced
Several threads saffron
1 teaspoon sunflower oil

1. Bring water and 1 teaspoon salt to a boil in a saucepan. Add rice, cover, and cook 17-20 minutes. When rice is done and water has been absorbed, spoon rice into a bowl.

2. In a large saucepan over medium heat, sauté garlic, scallion, and onion in olive oil until onion is translucent. Transfer to another bowl.

3. In the same pot, heat on medium-high, coconut milk, curry leaves, ginger, and turmeric. Add the sautéed ingredients, parsley, saffron, and sunflower oil. As soon as the coconut milk begins to boil, add the cooked rice and bring the mixture to a boil. Turn down the heat to a simmer. Cook with no cover for 12-15 minutes more minutes.

4. Serve warm.

Yellow Bean Eggplant

yield 2 servings

3 tablespoons olive oil

2 cloves garlic, crushed and cut into pieces

1 eggplant, cut into $1/4$-inch slices

2 red chile peppers, seeded and chopped

1 tablespoon chopped fresh basil leaves

$1/8$ teaspoon dill

2 tablespoons yellow bean sauce (found in Oriental markets)

1 scallion, chopped

$1/8$ cup green pepper, chopped

1 cup fresh tomatoes, diced

$1/2$ cup yogurt (goat yogurt preferred)

Basil for garnish

1.   Heat oil in wok over high heat. Add garlic and sauté until light brown.

2.   Add eggplant to wok and cook for 5 minutes. Stir in chiles, basil, dill, bean sauce, scallion, green pepper, and tomatoes. Mix well. Serve immediately, topped with a dollop of yogurt and a sprinkle of basil.

Positively Pea Pilaf

yield 2 servings

2 tablespoons walnut oil
2 shallots, finely chopped
1 clove garlic, minced
3/4 cup white basmati jasmine rice, rinsed and drained
1 1/3 cup vegetable broth

1/3 cup chopped fresh spearmint
1/2 cup frozen peas
1 tablespoon Bragg's liquid aminos, or to taste
Spinach, cooked Arugla (optional)

1.   In a stockpot, carefully heat walnut oil over low heat and sauté shallots and garlic for 3 minutes.

2.   Add uncooked rice and stir 1 minute.

3.   Add vegetable broth, spearmint, peas, and aminos. Bring to a full boil, then reduce heat to a simmer. Cover and cook over low heat approximately 15 minutes.

4.   Remove from heat. Release steam by angling lid away from face and hands. Cover with a towel to absorb excess water vapor without losing heat.

5.   Serve on a bed of spinach or arugla with olive oil.

Bread Hoops

yield 6 portions

1 tablespoon rapid rise yeast

1 teaspoon sea salt

2 cups spelt flour

2 cups rice flour

1/4 cup egg substitute

1 tablespoon mild honey

1 tablespoon sesame oil plus additional to brush tops of bread

3/4 cup rice milk

3/4 cup water

2 tablespoons minced garlic, sautéed lightly

1/2 cup sesame seeds lightly roasted in 1 tablespoon Braggs liquid aminos

1.   In a large bowl, mix the yeast, salt, flours, and egg substitute.

2.   In a deep pan, heat the honey, sesame oil, rice milk, and water to a temperature of 110°. (Check with candy thermometer.)

3.   Blend wet and dry ingredients, and add the garlic and 1/4 cup of the sesame seeds. Knead well, either with oiled hands or in a bread machine. Add more flour or water if needed to make a smooth, elastic dough that pulls away from the sides of the bowl.

4.   Divide dough into halves; divide each half into 3 portions. On an oiled or floured surface, roll each portion into a long rope.

5.   Connect the ends of each rope, forming 6 open donuts. Moisten fingertips in a few drops of water and seal the ends by pinching together.

6.   Brush tops with sesame oil, and press remaining 1/4 cup sesame seeds equally into each of the 6 ropes.

7. Place on lightly oiled cookie sheets, allowing space for dough to double in size. Let stand in warm spot away from drafts for about 30 minutes.

8. When doubling is complete, bake in preheated 350° oven until golden brown, approximately 15 minutes.

Chapter 5

MAIN DISHES

Algerian

Algerian Chili

Fish Couscous

Tuna and String Bean
Ragout

Tuna, Eggplant, and Chick
Pea Stew

Vegetable Medley

Brazilian

Black Bean Stew

Fish, Rio de Janeiro-style
with Shrimp Sauce

Red Snapper in Coconut
Milk

Vatapa

Chinese

Fish Chow Mein

Chop Suey

Lemon Swordfish

Lo Mein with Tempeh and
Bean Sprouts

Sweet and Sour Tempeh

Tofu with Broccoli

Sweet and Pungent Sea Bass

Sliced Tofu with Garlic
Sauce

Cuban

Fish with Rice

Swordfish Enchilado

English

Fish and Chips

Good Shepherd's Pie

Filipino

Sautéed Vegetables with
Noodles

Sesame and Spice Seitan

French

Ratatouille

German

Goulash

Marinated Roast Swordfish

Greek

Greek Smoked Eggplant

Greek Seafarer

Hungarian

Cauliflower with Shitake
Mushrooms

Eggplant Goulash

Paprika Swordfish

Sauerkraut Pockets

Stuffed Head of Cabbage

Indian

Indian Ratatouille

Potato Masala Curry

Rice and Lentils (Dahl)

Indonesian

Dijon Fish, Noodles, and
Vegetables

Irish

Collards and Potatoes

Cucumber Trout

Mock Meatball Veggie Stew

Italian

Spaghetti with Garlic and
Oil

Linguine with White
Tempeh Sauce

Fettuccine with Salmon

Eggplant Parmigiana Elinia

Pesto a la Mariano

Marsala Salmon

Neapolitan Salmon
Portabello

Northern Italian Baked Ziti
with Portabello

Vegetarian Lasagna

Tempeh Cacciatora Sauce

Jamaican

Almost Locrio Stew

Disappearing Codfish

Tamarindo Jerked Sturgeon

Jerked Fish

Codfish and Ackee

Curried Halibut

Jamaican Run Down

Turned Down Cornmeal

Mexican

Mexican Spicy Burritos

Burrito with Refried Beans
and Chili

Vegetarian Chili

Veracruz-style Red Snapper

Portuguese

Curried Salmon

Exotic Rice

Puerto Rican

Corn Pie

Salmon

Spanish Rice with Fish, Tofu,
and "No-Meatballs"

Spanish

Rice with Tempeh

Spanish Potato Omelet

Tempeh in Sherry Sauce

Thai

Sizzling Shrimp

Minted Pine Nut Curry

Mock Meatballs in Peanut
Sauce

Noodles Deluxe

Turkish

Pomegranate-stuffed
Eggplants

Algerian Chili

yield 2 servings

2 cups small dried navy beans

1/8 cup extra-virgin olive oil

1 medium onion, finely chopped

1 scallion, finely chopped

1 1/2 small dried red chiles

8 cloves garlic, minced

1/2 tablespoon sweet paprika

1/8 teaspoon freshly ground black pepper

1 tablespoon minced green bell pepper

1 tablespoon curry powder

2 teaspoons ground cumin

5 sundried tomatoes, reconstituted and puréed to generate 1/2 cup tomato paste

1 tomato, coarsely chopped

3 1/2 cups water or vegetable broth

1 bay leaf

Pinch of cayenne

10 fresh flat-leaf parsley sprigs, half tied together with kitchen string, half minced

1 1/4 teaspoons sea salt

5 fresh cilantro sprigs, chopped

1. Soak the dried beans overnight. Drain and set aside.

2. Over medium heat in a large soup pot, heat the oil and cook the onion and scallions, stirring occasionally, until tender, 6-8 minutes.

3. Add the chiles, garlic, paprika, pepper, green pepper, curry powder, and cumin. Cook, stirring, for 2-3 minutes and then add the sundried tomato paste and cook, stirring until the mixture thickens, 1-2 minutes. Stir in the fresh tomato and 1 cup of the water or broth and bring to a boil.

4. Add the beans and the remaining 2 1/2 cups water or broth, bay leaves, cayenne, sea salt, and the parsley bundle. Lower the heat to medium-low, cover and cook until the beans are tender, 1-2 hours.

5. Discard the chiles, bay leaves, and tied parsley before serving. Stir in the minced parsley and cilantro. Serve warm.

Fish Couscous

yield 2 servings

1 pound flounder or cod, cubed

1 small onion , chopped ($^1/2$ cup)

1 scallion, chopped

1 garlic clove, chopped

1 tablespoon diced green pepper

$^1/4$ cup cooked chick peas

2 carrots, peeled and sliced $^1/4$ inch thick

3 sprigs flat-leaf parsley, chopped

$1^1/2$ sprigs fresh coriander, chopped

$^1/4$ teaspoon sea salt, or to taste

$^1/8$ teaspoon freshly ground black pepper

$^1/8$ teaspoon turmeric

$^1/8$ teaspoon ground cinnamon

$^1/8$ teaspoon nutmeg

1 teaspoon olive oil

$1^2/3$ cups water

$10^1/2$ ounces couscous

1.   Put all ingredients except water and couscous in a large saucepan and stir fry over low heat for 15 minutes.

2.   Add the water, bring to a boil, and cook over moderate heat for 45 minutes.

3.   Prepare couscous in a separate saucepan according to the package directions.

4.   Spoon the fish and vegetables over the couscous and serve.

Tuna and String Bean Ragout

yield 2 servings

1 1/2 tablespoons extra-virgin olive oil

1 pound tuna cut into 1-inch cubes

1 vidalia onion, 1/2 chopped and 1/2 sliced into rounds

1 scallion, chopped

2 cloves garlic, minced

1 tablespoon minced green bell pepper

1/2 teaspoon sea salt

1/8 teaspoon freshly ground black pepper

1 teaspoon ground cumin, divided

1/2 teaspoon curry powder

1/4 teaspoon hot red chili powder

1/4 teaspoon turmeric

2 cups water

2 cups fresh string beans, cut into 2-inch pieces

1 ripe tomato, sliced into rounds

1 sprig flat-leaf parsley, chopped

1. Heat the oil in a large saucepan and add tuna, onion, scallion, garlic, and green pepper. Sauté over low heat for 3-5 minutes, until onions are slightly clear.

2. Add salt, pepper, 1/2 teaspoon of the cumin, curry powder, chili powder, turmeric, and water. Bring to a boil and simmer over low heat for 45 minutes.

3. Add the string beans and cook for 15 minutes.

4. Add the sliced onion and tomatoes and sprinkle the remaining 1/2 teaspoon of cumin and the parsley over the ragout sauce. Simmer for 15 minutes without stirring.

5. Serve hot.

Tuna, Eggplant, and Chick Pea Stew

yield 2 servings

1 tablespoon olive oil

1 pound tuna steaks

1 medium onion, chopped (about 1/2 cup)

1 1/2 eggplants cut crosswise into 1/2-inch slices

2 medium potatoes, peeled and sliced in 1/4-inch rounds

1 teaspoon white pepper

1/4 teaspoon saffron stamens or 1/4 teaspoon turmeric

1/2 teaspoon sea salt

1/3 cup dried chick peas, soaked in water overnight and drained

1 1/2 cups water

2 medium cloves garlic

3/4 teaspoons ground caraway seeds

1 tablespoon honey

1. Put the oil in a pan with tuna and onion. Stir fry over low heat for 5 minutes until the onion becomes translucent.

2. Add the eggplant, potatoes, pepper, saffron, and salt and continue to cook for an additional 5 minutes. Add the chick peas and water and bring to a boil. Cover and cook over low heat for 1 1/2 hours.

3. Crush the garlic and caraway together in a mortar and stir into the stew. Add the honey. Simmer for 5 minutes more and remove from heat.

Vegetable Medley

yield 2 servings

1 tablespoon olive oil

1/2 onion, diced, plus
1 teaspoon minced
onion for garnish

4 cloves garlic, pressed
through garlic press

3/4 cup peeled and diced
eggplant

6 okra, sliced into 1/4-inch
circles

1 teaspoon paprika

1 tablespoon minced parsley

1/2 cup peeled and diced
carrots

1 cup peeled and diced sweet
potato

1/2 cup uncooked millet

1 cup fresh fava beans, cut
into bite size

1/2 cup green beans, cut into
bite size

1 1/2 cups vegetable broth

1/8 teaspoon periperi sauce

Sea salt to taste

Freshly ground black pepper
to taste

1 small, white onion, minced

1. Heat oil over medium heat in a large saucepan. Cook onion, garlic, eggplant, and okra approximately 5 minutes.

2. Add paprika and parsley. Stir to blend.

3. Add carrots, potato, millet, fava beans, green beans, and vegetable broth. Cover and continue cooking 30 minutes.

4. Season to taste with periperi sauce, sea salt, and pepper. Garnish with minced onions.

Black Bean Stew

yield 2 servings

1 cup dried or 2 cups cooked
   black beans

1 tablespoon olive oil

1 large onion, diced

2 cloves garlic, crushed

1 red bell pepper, diced

2 cups water

1 tablespoon cayenne

1 scallion, diced

2 tomatoes, blanched, peeled,
   and diced

1 bay leaf

Freshly ground black pepper
   to taste

1 tablespoon Braggs liquid
   aminos or sea salt to taste

Chili powder to taste

Bouquet garni: 3-5 shallots
   and a small bunch of
   parsley tied together in
   a cheesecloth sack

SPICY SAUCE

1 scallion, diced

1 onion, diced

1 red chile, finely chopped

$1/2$ teaspoon apple cider
   vinegar

Juice of 1 lemon

Sea salt to taste

1 shallot, chopped

2 tablespoons olive oil

12 sprigs parsley, chopped

1 tablespoon Bragg's liquid
   aminos

1 tablespoon cayenne

Brown rice, cooked

1.   If using dried beans, soak overnight and cook in plenty of water until tender, about 1 hour.

2.   In a large stockpot over medium heat, heat the oil and sauté the onion, garlic, and bell pepper until onion is golden. Add water, cayenne, scallion, tomatoes, bay leaf, black pepper, Braggs or sea salt, chili powder, and the bouquet garni. Bring the mixture to a boil.

3.   Reduce heat to low and simmer for about 15 minutes, then add half the cooked beans. Mash together well in the pot (avoiding the garni), then add the remaining cooked beans and continue cooking until the liquid thickens. Taste for seasoning and remove the bouquet garni.

4.   *To prepare the sauce*: Place all ingredients in a bowl. Add a ladle of strained liquid from the stew. Stir to combine thoroughly.

5.   Serve with brown rice and a dollop of Spicy Sauce.

Fish Rio de Janeiro-style with Shrimp Sauce

yield 2 servings

FISH
1 pound fresh fillet of codfish
$1/2$ cup chopped onion
1 clove garlic, minced
$1/4$ teaspoon paprika
$1/2$ teaspoon sea salt

DOUGH
2 teaspoons peanut oil
$1/2$ cup spelt flour
$1/4$ teaspoon sea salt
2 tablespoons water
$1/4$ cup egg substitute
1 tablespoon soy milk powder

PRAWN SAUCE
$1/2$ pound prawns
1 small onion, chopped
$1/2$ cup fresh tomato, seeded, peeled, and chopped
1 tablespoon avocado or olive oil
$3/4$ cup reserved fish cooking water
2 teaspoons spelt flour
2 sundried tomatoes, reconstituted and puréed
$1/8$ teaspoon sea salt

GARNISH
$1/2$ cup hearts of palm

1. *To season the fish:* Place fish in a medium saucepan with enough water to cover. Add the onion, garlic, paprika, and $1/2$ teaspoon sea salt. Simmer for 15 minutes.

2. Remove fish, discard the skin, and break the flesh into large flakes. Reserve cooking water.

3. *To prepare the dough:* Preheat oven to 350°. Mix peanut oil with spelt flour, salt, water, egg substitute, and soy milk powder. Add more water if needed.

4. Roll out to $1/4$-inch thickness, and cut into strips measuring 1 inch × 4 inches. Cut off the corners of one end of each, creating a point.

5. Place the strips of dough on a lightly oiled baking sheet and bake until golden, 17-20 minutes.

6. *To prepare the sauce:* Wash, shell, and devein prawns.

7. Sauté onion and tomato in 1 teaspoon of the avocado oil over medium-low heat for 7-10 minutes.

8. Return prawns to pan, adding ¾ cup fish water. Cook 7 minutes. Remove prawns and set aside.

9. To thicken the liquid, add flour, remaining oil, sundried tomato purée, and salt. Simmer until sauce thickens.

10. *To garnish*, place cod in center of platter, surrounded with hearts of palm. Cover with sauce and arrange pastry points and prawns in a decorative manner.

Red Snapper in Coconut Milk

yield 2 servings

2 small onions, peeled and chopped

2 cloves garlic, minced

3/4 teaspoon sea salt

Juice of 1 lime

1 red snapper fillet

1 large plantain, peeled, sliced, and boiled until very soft

1/4 cup pumpkin seed or olive oil

1 cup thick coconut milk

1/8 teaspoon cinnamon

1 teaspoon honey

1 red bell pepper, seeded and cut into thin strips

1 tablespoon palm or peanut oil

Sea salt to taste

White pepper to taste

1/3 cup water

2 tablespoons spelt flour

Lime wedges for garnish

1 tablespoon parsley

1. In a large bowl, mix together half the chopped onions, half the minced garlic, salt, and lime juice. Place fillets in the bowl and cover with plastic wrap. Marinate the fillets overnight in refrigerator.

2. In a blender, purée the boiled soft plantain with the pumpkin seed oil, half the coconut milk, cinnamon, and honey.

3. In a pan, sauté the remaining onion and garlic and the red pepper in the palm oil over low heat. Season with sea salt and pepper.

4. Remove fillets from the marinade and drain. Discard the marinade.

5. In the bottom of a steamer, combine the remaining 1/2 cup coconut milk and 1/3 cup hot water. Steam the snapper 7-10 minutes, or until the fish is opaque and flakes when probed with a fork. Remove cooked snapper to a serving platter.

6.　In a small bowl, combine 2 tablespoons spelt flour with a little cold water. Stir this mixture into the water-coconut mixture and stir continuously until it thickens.

7.　Whisk the sauce together with the plantain purée until heated through, and drizzle over the fish. Top with the onion-garlic-red pepper mixture, and garnish with lime wedges and fresh parsley.

Vatapa

yield 2 servings

3 slices rice bread or almond
bread (available at health
food stores)
3/4 cup coconut milk
1/2 cup chopped onion
1 clove garlic, minced
1/2 teaspoon paprika
1/8 teaspoon cayenne
1/2 teaspoon chopped
cilantro

1/2 teaspoon sea salt
1/2 teaspoon minced ginger
1 pound fresh shrimp
1/2 cup brazil nuts, toasted
and finely chopped
1/3 cup cashew, finely
chopped
1/3 cup peanut oil

1.   Trim crusts from bread and discard. Break bread into pieces
and put into a bowl.

2.   Pour 1/3 cup of the coconut milk over the bread and set aside
to soften.

3.   Mash the bread mixture with a fork until fine. Add onion,
garlic, paprika, cayenne, cilantro, salt, and ginger, and mix well.

4.   Preheat oven to 325°.

5.   Spread the shrimp on a cookie sheet and bake them in the
oven until dry, approximately 1 hour depending upon size.

6.   Remove the shells and grind or purée shrimp until they
reach a powdery consistency. Combine with the brazil nuts and
cashews.

7.   In a large saucepan, combine shrimp/nut mixture with bread mixture. Stir in the remaining coconut milk.

8.   Cook over medium-low heat, stirring constantly in clockwise direction until thick, about 5 minutes. Add salt to taste.

9.   Mix in peanut oil and remove from heat. Serve warm.

Fish Chow Mein

yield 2 servings

MARINADE

1/4 teaspoon rice vinegar

3/4 teaspoon powdered arrowroot

1/4 teaspoon sea salt

1/2 tablespoon canola oil

TO CONTINUE THE RECIPE

1/4 pound mild white fish fillet (such as halibut, cod, or sole), cubed

4 cups water

4 ounces dry Chinese noodles or angel hair spaghetti

1/2 tablespoon sesame oil

1/3 cup canola oil

1/4 cup shredded bamboo shoots

1/2 cup fresh mung bean sprouts or 1/2 cup shredded cabbage

1/2 cup sliced fresh mushrooms

1/4 cup shredded onion

1/2 clove elephant garlic or 2 cloves garlic, minced

1 1/2 tablespoons vegetable broth

1/4 teaspoon sea salt

TO COMPLETE THE RECIPE

1 1/2 tablespoons tamari sauce

Pinch freshly ground black pepper

1. *To prepare the marinade*: Combine rice vinegar, arrowroot, salt, and oil in a small bowl.

2. *To continue the recipe*: Cut the fish into cubes and add it to the marinade. Mix well and allow to stand 30 minutes.

3. Meanwhile, bring water to a boil in a large saucepan and cook noodles until tender. Rinse with cold water, drain well, and add sesame oil. Mix well to coat, and set aside.

4. Heat 1/8 cup of the canola oil in a wok over medium heat for 1 minute. Stir-fry fish until cooked, about 1-2 minutes. Remove fish with a slotted spoon, drain well over wok and set aside.

5. Add $^1/_2$ tablespoon of oil to wok, and heat 30 seconds over high heat. Add bamboo shoots, bean sprouts or cabbage, mushrooms, onions, and garlic, and stir-fry 3 minutes.

6. Add vegetable broth and sea salt to vegetables. If mixture seems too dry, add more water or broth. Remove vegetables from wok and set aside.

7. Reduce the heat to medium and add $1^1/_2$ tablespoons oil to wok. Stir-fry cooked noodles 3-4 minutes.

8. *To complete the recipe*: Add tamari sauce, pepper, vegetables, and fish to wok. Stir-fry 2 minutes longer, mixing well. Serve hot.

Chop Suey

yield 2 servings

SAUCE

1 teaspoon honey

1 cup vegetable broth, or 1 vegetable bouillon cube dissolved in 1 cup water

1 teaspoon tamari sauce

2 teaspoons rice vinegar

1¹/2 tablespoons arrowroot powder

1 tablespoon cider vinegar

VEGETABLES

2 teaspoons sesame oil

1 clove garlic, minced

¹/2 cup bamboo shoots from can, rinsed, drained, and sliced

1 head bok choy, stems sliced diagonally, leaves thinly sliced

2 cups chopped cauliflower

³/4 cup diagonally sliced celery

1 cup sliced straw mushrooms

1 cup bean sprouts, preferably mung bean, rinsed

¹/2 cup tamari almonds, sliced

1. *To prepare the sauce:* In a small saucepan, heat honey, broth, tamari sauce, and rice vinegar.

2. In a bowl, whisk together arrowroot and cider vinegar.

3. *To prepare the vegetables:* Heat sesame oil in wok. Add garlic, bamboo shoots, bok choy stems, cauliflower, and celery, and stir-fry 4 minutes. Add mushrooms, bean sprouts, and bok choy leaves. Stir-fry 2 more minutes. Empty wok into a large bowl.

4. Combine honey-tamari mixture with arrowroot sauce in middle of wok and stir constantly until sauce thickens and loses cloudiness.

5. Gently stir in vegetables and reheat for 2 minutes.

6. Garnish with tamari almonds.

Lemon Swordfish

yield 2 servings

1 tablespoon apple cider
   vinegar

2 teaspoons dry sherry

2 teaspoons golden miso

6 ounces skinless swordfish
   fillet, cut into 3/4-inch
   strips

1 tablespoon arrowroot
   powder

1/4 cup frozen lemonade
   concentrate

2 tablespoons safflower oil

1 teaspoon freshly minced
   ginger

1 tablespoon minced fresh
   garlic

1 tablespoon lemon zest

2 scallions, sliced into thin
   slivers 1 1/2 inches long

1 carrot, cut into 1/2-inch
   slivers

1/2 green bell pepper, cleaned
   and cut into 1 1/2-inch
   slivers

Canola spray

1 tablespoon freshly
   squeezed lemon juice

1 1/2 cups finely shredded
   crisp lettuce

1/2 lemon, sliced thinly

1. Combine cider vinegar, sherry, and golden miso in a bowl.
Add swordfish strips and marinate 30-60 minutes. Remove fish and
reserve marinade.

2. In a blender, combine marinade with arrowroot powder and
lemonade concentrate until smooth.

3. Heat oil in a wok. Stir-fry ginger, garlic, swordfish, lemon zest,
scallions, carrot, and pepper for 3 minutes. Remove and set aside.

4. Rinse out wok and reheat for 30 seconds. Spray lightly with
canola spray. Pour arrowroot-lemonade into the wok. Heat until thickened, then return swordfish and vegetables to wok. Toss gently to coat.

5. Stir in fresh lemon juice and serve immediately on a platter
on top of shredded lettuce. Garnish with thinly sliced lemon rounds,
twisted to affect a swirl.

Lo Mein with Tempeh and Bean Sprouts

yield 2 servings

2 large or 3 small dried black
  mushrooms
Boiling water
2-2$^1/2$ cups bean sprouts
$^1/4$ pound rice noodles
$^1/2$ cup celery cabbage,
  shredded crosswise
1 cup tempeh
$^1/8$ teaspoon date sugar

$^1/4$ teaspoon sea salt
$^1/2$ tablespoon shao hsing
  wine or dry sherry
$^1/8$ cup canola oil
2 teaspoons tamari, divided
$^1/4$ cup vegetable broth
$^1/4$ cup chives cut into 1-inch
  lengths

1. Place mushrooms in a mixing bowl and add enough boiling water to cover. Let stand 20 minutes, then drain and squeeze out excess moisture. Discard the tough stems.

2. Rinse and drain bean sprouts, and set aside.

3. Cook noodles according to package directions. Rinse under cold water and set aside.

4. Shred the mushrooms and put them in the bowl. There should be about $^1/8$ cup.

5. Add the cabbage to the mushrooms.

6. Cut the tempeh into cubes. This is easier to do if tempeh is partially frozen.

7. In a small bowl, combine the date sugar, salt, and wine and set aside.

8. In a wok or skillet heat, 1 tablespoon of the oil. When hot, add the tempeh, stirring to separate the pieces. Add 1/2 teaspoon of the tamari and cook, stirring, about 30 seconds. Drain.

9. Add the remaining oil to the pan, then the cabbage and mushrooms. Cook, stirring, for about 1 minute.

10. Add the noodles and cook over high heat tossing ingredients together. Cook another minute, stirring, then add wine mixture.

11. Add vegetable broth and cook, stirring, about 30 seconds. Add the remaining tamari and cook, stirring, about 3 minutes.

12. Toss in bean sprouts and chives, and serve hot.

O p t i o n a l *If you wish, combine 1/8 cup apple cider vinegar and 1/2 teaspoon or more chile oil to use as a sauce.*

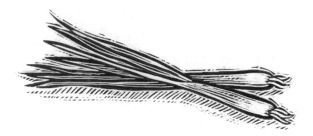

Sweet and Sour Tempeh

yield 2 servings

1/2 tablespoon tamari

1/2 tablespoon white wine (Sauvignon Blanc is preferred)

1/2 cup plus 1 tablespoon arrowroot

1/2 pound tempeh, cut into 3/4-inch cubes

2 dried black mushrooms

Boiling water

1/4 cup green and red bell peppers cut into 1-inch cubes

1 tablespoon sliced carrot

1/2 cup onion cut into 1-inch cubes

1/8 cup thinly sliced bamboo shoots

1/4 cup drained pineapple chunks or sliced pineapple cut into bite-size pieces

1/4 cup pickled scallions, each cut in half

2 cloves garlic, peeled and crushed, and left whole

2 thin slices fresh ginger, peeled

Oil for deep frying

3/4 cup water

2 tablespoons golden honey

1/4 cup apple cider vinegar

1/2 tablespoon light or golden miso paste (available at health food stores)

Sea salt to taste

4 Red Zinger tea bags for steeping (available at health food stores)

8 cups water

Walnut oil

1.   In a bowl, mix the tamari and wine.

2.   Place 1/2 cup of the arrowroot on a large sheet of waxed paper and dredge the tempeh in it, one piece at a time. Gently massage each piece to coat well. Throw away leftover arrowroot.

3.   Place the mushrooms in a mixing bowl and add enough boiling water to cover. Let stand 15 minutes or until softened.

4.   In a mixing bowl, combine the pepper cubes, carrot, onion, bamboo shoots, pineapple, scallions, garlic, and ginger.

5. Drain the mushrooms and squeeze to extract the moisture. Cut off and discard the stems and slice the mushrooms thinly. Add the mushrooms to the other vegetables and set aside.

6. In a wok, heat to the boiling point oil for deep frying. Drop the dusted tempeh pieces, several at a time, into the oil. Cook 5-7 minutes, or until the tempeh is golden brown and crisp. Remove and drain on paper towels.

7. Drain off all except $1/8$ cup of the oil, cup and add the vegetable mixture. Cook, stirring, 4-5 minutes.

8. Meanwhile, in a saucepan, combine $1/2$ cup of the water, honey, apple cider vinegar, light miso paste, and sea salt and bring to a boil. Stir until smooth.

9. Steep 4 Red Zinger tea bags in a small pot with 8 cups of water for 10-15 minutes. Remove tea bags, and squeeze the color out of the tea bags. Add the $1/8$ cup of red liquid to the remaining 1 tablespoon of arrowroot. Stir in 1 tablespoon of fresh walnut oil to glaze the sauce. Pour the sauce over the vegetables and bring to a boil.

10. Transfer the tempeh to a serving dish. Pour the vegetable sauce over the tempeh and serve.

Tofu with Broccoli

yield 2 servings

MARINADE

1/4 teaspoon baking soda

1/2 tablespoon tamari sauce

1/2 tablespoon sesame oil

1/8 teaspoon honey

3/4 teaspoon powdered or granulated lecithin

1/8 cup water

TO CONTINUE THE RECIPE

1/3 pound firm or extra-firm tofu, sliced into medium thin strips

1/4 pound broccoli tops

1 teaspoon powdered arrow-root

3 1/2 tablespoons canola oil

1 small garlic clove, crushed

TO COMPLETE THE RECIPE

1/2 teaspoon sea salt

1/4 teaspoon tamari sauce

1 1/2 tablespoons vegetable broth

1/8 teaspoon pepper plus 1/8 teaspoon cayenne

Sesame seeds (optional)

1. *To prepare the marinade*: Mix marinade ingredients in a medium bowl.

2. *To continue the recipe*: Add tofu strips. Mix gently and let stand 30 minutes.

3. Cut each broccoli top lengthwise into 2 or 3 pieces.

4. Dissolve arrowroot in sufficient water to make a smooth paste; set aside.

5. Heat 3 tablespoons oil in a wok over high heat for 1 minute. Stir-fry marinated tofu until very lightly browned. Remove tofu, draining well over wok. Set aside.

6. Add 1/2 tablespoon oil to oil left in wok. Heat 30 seconds, then stir-fry garlic 30 seconds.

7. Add broccoli tops, stir-fry 5 minutes.

8. *To complete the recipe*: Add arrowroot paste, sea salt, tamari sauce, vegetable broth, and pepper. Stir-fry until sauce thickens slightly.

9. Add cooked tofu, and mix well. Remove from wok and arrange on a platter.

10. If you like, sauté sesame seeds in minimal oil and sprinkle on platter before serving.

VARIATION

After stir-frying broccoli, add tofu. Stir-fry tofu and broccoli
30 seconds to mix well. Mound on a plate or in a bowl to serve.

Sweet and Pungent Sea Bass

yield 2 servings

MARINADE

1¹/2 tablespoons arrowroot powder, divided

1 egg white, slightly beaten with 1 teaspoon sea salt

2 tablespoons sesame oil, divided

1 tablespoon low-sodium soy sauce

8-ounce fillet of sea bass, cut into ³/4-inch cubes

SAUCE

1¹/2 tablespoons dry sherry

1 tablespoon frozen orange juice concentrate

1 tablespoon frozen cranberry juice concentrate

1 tablespoon honey

1 tablespoon ketchup

2¹/2 tablespoons apple cider vinegar

TO COMPLETE THE RECIPE

Canola oil spray

1 teaspoon minced garlic

1 teaspoon minced ginger

³/4 cup chopped red bell pepper

³/4 cup chopped green bell pepper

1 cup cubed fresh pineapple

¹/2 cup chopped vidalia onion

10 fresh cherries, pitted and cut in half

1. *To prepare the marinade*: Dissolve ¹/2 tablespoon arrowroot powder, egg white, 1 tablespoon sesame oil, and soy sauce. Mix well.

2. Marinate sea bass 30-45 minutes in the soy sauce mixture.

3. *To prepare the sauce*: In a saucepan, combine sherry, orange juice and cranberry concentrates, honey, ketchup, and remaining 1 tablespoon arrowroot powder and 1 tablespoon sesame oil. Heat until glossy, about 3-4 minutes, stirring frequently. Stir in vinegar and set aside.

4. *To complete the recipe*: Heat nonstick wok on high. Spray with canola oil. Remove sea bass from the marinade. Discard marinade. Stir-fry sea bass 2-3 minutes. Remove from wok and carefully wipe with a paper towel.

5.   Respray wok and reheat. Add garlic and ginger. Stir-fry 1 minute.

6.   Add peppers, pineapple, and onion. Stir-fry 2 minutes.

7.   Combine sea bass with vegetables in the wok. Drizzle sauce over top and add cherries. Serve with white basmati rice on the side.

Sliced Tofu with Garlic Sauce

y i e l d   2   s e r v i n g s

TOFU

2 cups water

1 slice fresh ginger, peeled

2 cups, approximately, extra firm tofu (block form)

3 scallions

1/2 teaspoon rice wine

1 clove garlic

GARLIC SAUCE

1 tablespoon Bragg's liquid aminos

1 tablespoon curry powder

1 tablespoon vegetable broth

1 tablespoon water

1 scallion, chopped

1 tablespoon minced garlic

1/8 teaspoon sea salt

1 tablespoon tamari

1 teaspoon sesame oil

1/2 teaspoon honey

1/2 tablespoon chile oil or sesame oil

1. *To prepare the tofu*: In a medium saucepan, bring water to a boil. Add ginger, tofu block, scallions, wine, and garlic. Cook about 30 minutes, adding more boiling water if necessary.

2. Remove tofu block from cooking liquid. Set aside the liquid. Refrigerate tofu to facilitate slicing. When cool, cut tofu into ribbon slices, then cut the slices into 2-inch squares.

3. *To prepare the sauce*: Bring aminos, curry powder, vegetable broth, and water to a boil in a small saucepan. Remove from heat. Add remaining ingredients, mixing well. Set aside.

4. Bring tofu cooking liquid to a boil. Place tofu slices in boiling liquid for about 5-7 seconds. Remove and drain. Pat dry with a paper towel.

5. Arrange tofu on a platter. Pour garlic sauce over tofu slices. Sprinkle with chile oil or sesame oil to taste.

Fish with Rice

yield 2 servings

2 tablespoons olive oil

1 pound talapia, cut into pieces

1/4 yellow onion, chopped

1 clove garlic, minced

1/4 green bell pepper, chopped

1/4 cup chopped, stewed tomatoes

1 tablespoon tamari

1/4 teaspoon freshly ground black pepper

1 bay leaf

1/4 cup sliced black olives

3 tablespoons fresh dill, chopped

1 teaspoon chile pepper

1 teaspoon salt

1 teaspoon cumin

2 teaspoons lemon juice

1/4 tablespoon paprika

2 cups dry white wine (chablis or pinot grigio)

1/2 cup uncooked Jasmine basmati white rice

3 tablespoons green peas

1/2 onion, chopped, for garnish

Orange, pepper slices, and carrot peels for garnish

1. Heat oil in skillet. Brown fish pieces and remove.

2. In the same oil, sauté the onion, garlic, and green pepper until onion is golden.

3. Add the tomatoes, tamari, black pepper, bay leaf, olives, dill, chile pepper, salt, cumin, lemon juice, and paprika. Simmer for 30 minutes.

4. Add the wine and rice and simmer for 20 minutes, until rice is tender.

5. Sprinkle peas and fish on top and cook 5 minutes more. Serve hot with onion sprinkled on top. Garnish with orange and pepper slices and carrot peels.

Swordfish Enchilado

yield 2 servings

MARINADE
1/4 cup lime juice
Pinch salt
Pinch freshly ground black
   pepper
Pinch dried chile flakes

TO CONTINUE THE RECIPE
1 pound swordfish, cubed
2 tablespoons olive oil
1/4 large red onion, chopped
1/4 green bell pepper,
   chopped

2 garlic cloves, minced

TO COMPLETE THE RECIPE
1/2 cup tomato sauce
2 tablespoons chopped
   pimientos with their liquid
3 tablespoons prepared
   mustard
1/4 teaspoon lemon pepper
   (or black pepper plus the
   zest of 1/2 lemon)
1 tablespoon chopped
   parsley

1.   *To prepare marinade*: Combine marinade ingredients in a large bowl.

2.   *To continue the recipe*: Add swordfish to the bowl and marinate for 1 hour.

3.   In large, deep skillet, sauté swordfish over medium heat in olive oil until fish is opaque and flakes when probed with fork. Remove with slotted spoon.

4.   In the same oil, sauté onion and green pepper until soft. Add garlic and cook 2 more minutes.

5.   Reduce heat to low and return swordfish cubes to the skillet.

6.   *To complete the recipe*, add tomato sauce, pimientos, mustard, lemon pepper, and parsley. Warm through and serve.

Fish and Chips

yield 2 servings

1 pound Yukon gold pota-
toes, peeled and sliced
into thin wedges

Sea salt

3/4 cup rice flour, plus extra
for dusting

1/2 teaspoon baking soda

1/4 teaspoon sea salt

1/4 teaspoon garlic powder

1/8 teaspoon curry powder

1/8 teaspoon ground white
pepper

1 teaspoon parsley flakes

1/2 cup beer (light beer
preferred)

1 pound whitefish fillets with
skin attached

2 tablespoons canola oil

1.   Preheat oven to 400°.

2.   Place the potato slices on a lightly oiled cookie sheet and sprinkle with sea salt. Bake until tender and lightly brown, about 30-45 minutes.

3.   In a small bowl, mix together flour, baking soda, salt, garlic powder, curry powder, pepper, and parsley flakes.

4.   Whisk together the beer with the dry ingredients until smooth. Add more flour or beer until firm consistency is achieved.

5.   Dry the fillets, then dust with flour. Generously cover the fish in batter.

6.   Heat the oil in a pan and sauté the fish until golden brown, approximately 2-3 minutes on each side. Drain on paper towels and serve with chips.

Good Shepherd's Pie

yield 2 servings

1 large baking potato, peeled and diced

2 tablespoons sunflower seed oil

1/2 cup rice milk (plain)

1 tablespoon curry powder

1/4 teaspoon celery salt

1/8 teaspoon freshly ground black pepper

1 tablespoon olive oil

1 clove garlic, minced

1 medium onion, chopped

1 scallion, chopped

1/2 pound vegetarian meat substitute (texturized vegetable protein, or TVP)

1 vegetable bouillon cube

3 ounces tomato paste

1/4 cup anchovy paste

1/8 teaspoon sage

1 tablespoon spelt flour

1 teaspoon parsley flakes

1 teaspoon dried tarragon

3/4 cup white wine (Liebfraumilch preferred)

1/2 can adzuki beans

Pinch of paprika

1. Cook potato in boiling, salted water. Drain and mash, and add the sunflower oil and rice milk. Season with curry powder, celery salt, and pepper.

2. Heat olive oil and sauté garlic, onion, and scallion until soft. Add the meat substitute and stir until brown and flavors are married, about 5 minutes.

3. Crumble the vegetable bouillon and stir it into onion mixture. Stir in tomato paste, anchovy paste, sage, flour, parsley, and tarragon leaves. Add the wine and continue stirring for a few minutes. Cover and simmer on low for 10 additional minutes.

4. Preheat oven to 350°. Lightly coat soufflé dish or bread pan with oil.

5. Spread onion mixture on bottom of the dish. Follow with a layer of cooked adzuki beans and then mashed potatoes, and sprinkle with paprika.

6. Bake for 30 minutes, then brown under broiler for 1 minute and serve.

Sautéed Vegetables with Noodles

yield 2 servings

¹/4 pound rice noodles

3 tablespoons olive oil

¹/2 tablespoon minced garlic

¹/4 cup sliced onion

¹/4 pound shiitake mush-
rooms

¹/4 pound seitan, cut into
bite size pieces and stir-
fried

¹/2 cup chang, thinly sliced

1 carrot, cut into matchstick
pieces or thinly sliced

¹/4 cup chopped scallions

¹/8 teaspoon cayenne

¹/4 teaspoon anise seed

¹/4 teaspoon cumin

¹/2 cup water

1 tablespoon soy sauce

1 tablespoon toasted sesame
oil

1 cup snow peas

1 cup fresh basil

Lemon pepper or black
pepper to taste

Lemon wedges and scallions
for garnish

1. Cook rice noodles according to the package instructions.

2. Strain the noodles, add 1 tablespoon of the olive oil, toss to coat, and set aside.

3. In a wok or large saucepan over high heat, sauté garlic and onion in remaining 2 tablespoons oil until translucent.

4. Stir in mushrooms and seitan.

5. Add chang, carrot, scallions, cayenne, anise seed, cumin, water, and soy sauce and cook until done, about 10 minutes.

6. Add noodles and sesame oil. Cook for 10 minutes.

7. Stir in snow peas and fresh basil.

8. Arrange on a large serving platter, and garnish with lemon pepper, lemon wedges, and scallions.

Sesame and Spice Seitan

yield 2 servings

2^1/2 cups water

1 cup basmati rice

^{1}/2 cup sweet peas

^{1}/4 tablespoon lemon or black peppercorns

4 teaspoons toasted sesame oil

1 pound seitan, cut into 1-inch cubes

4 cloves garlic, crushed

1 teaspoon celery seed

1 teaspoon dill

1 teaspoon mustard seed

Sea salt to taste

Orange wedges for garnish

1. Bring a large pot of water to a boil. Add rice and simmer, covered, for 40 minutes or until rice is done. Season with sweet peas and peppercorns.

2. As the rice is cooking, heat the oil in the wok over high heat. Add the seitan and cook for 5 minutes. Add the garlic, celery seed, dill, mustard seed, and salt, and cook 5 minutes more.

3. Mix rice and seasoned seitan together. Serve warm, decorated with orange wedges around the edges of the plate.

Ratatouille

yield 2 servings

1/2 cup olive oil, divided

1 small eggplant, peeled and cubed

1 small yellow squash, cubed

1/4 cup minced shallots

1 scallion, chopped

2 cloves garlic, pressed

1 small zucchini, cubed

1/4 teaspoon dried thyme

1 tablespoon freshly chopped basil

1/2 onion, chopped

2 tablespoons minced dulse leaves

1/2 stalk celery, chopped

1/2 cup sundried tomatoes, reconstituted in 1/2 cup water

1 teaspoon curry powder

Sea salt to taste

Freshly ground black pepper to taste

1/4 cup sunflower seeds

1. Heat 1/4 cup olive oil in a large skillet over medium heat. Add eggplant, yellow squash, shallots, scallion, garlic, and zucchini. Add thyme, basil, onion, dulse, and celery.

2. Place the reconstituted sundried tomatoes, remaining 1/4 cup olive oil, and curry powder in a blender and purée.

3. Preheat oven to 350°.

4. Transfer the contents of the skillet and the blender into a lightly oiled 1 quart baking dish or Dutch oven, and toss lightly. Flavor with salt and pepper. Sprinkle top with sunflower seeds and bake for 35 minutes. Serve hot.

Goulash

yield 2 servings

1 tablespoon olive oil

1 medium onion, chopped

2 shallots, chopped

1 stalk celery, chopped

1 medium tomato, chopped

$1/8$ cup honey (orange flavored is best)

$3/4$ cup firm tofu, crumbled

Sea salt to taste

$1/4$ teaspoon caraway seeds

$1/2$ teaspoon paprika

1 cup plus 1 tablespoon water

1 teaspoon dark, unsulphured molasses

1 tablespoon Braggs liquid aminos

1 tablespoon arrowroot powder

Freshly ground black pepper to taste

$1/3$ cup soft or silken tofu

Pinch of paprika

1. Heat the oil over medium-high heat, and sauté onions, shallots, celery, and tomato until caramelized, about 5 minutes.

2. Add honey and crumbled firm tofu, and sprinkle mixture with sea salt, caraway seeds, and paprika.

3. Add $1/2$ cup of water. Cover and simmer for $1/2$ hour.

4. In a blender, mix $1/2$ cup water, molasses, aminos, and arrowroot. Pour over vegetable-tofu mixture and stir until thickened. Season to taste with sea salt and pepper.

5. Purée the soft or silken tofu in a blender with one tablespoon of water until creamy. Serve the goulash topped with a dollop of creamed tofu and a pinch of paprika.

Marinated Roast Swordfish

yield 2 servings

MARINADE
1/4 cup balsamic vinegar
1 cup water
1 onion, sliced
1 clove garlic, minced
1 bay leaf
3 French or black pepper-
    corns, crushed
2 cloves
1/2 teaspoon sea salt
1 teaspoon grated fresh or
    3/4 teaspoon ground
    ginger
2 tablespoons soy sauce

TO CONTINUE THE RECIPE
1 pound fresh swordfish
    fillet, skinned

TOFU CREAM
1/3 cup soft tofu
2 teaspoons fresh lemon juice
3/4 teaspoon ume vinegar,
    optional

TO COMPLETE THE RECIPE
2 teaspoons pine nut oil
2 tablespoons soy or rice
    flour
1/3 cup water

1. *To prepare the marinade*: In a saucepan, combine and heat marinade ingredients until boiling. Remove from heat and cool to room temperature.

2. *To continue the recipe*: Place swordfish in bowl and cover with marinade. Cover and refrigerate for 1 day, turning the fish over throughout the day.

3. *To prepare tofu cream*: In a blender, combine the tofu, lemon juice, and vinegar.

4. Remove fish from marinade. Strain and reserve marinade.

5. *To complete the recipe*: In a sauté pan, heat the oil over high heat. Sear the swordfish, about 30 seconds on each side.

6.   Add ⅔ cup marinade to fish, cover, and simmer on low for one-half hour, adding water if necessary to maintain level.

7.   Mix flour with ⅓ cup water and remaining marinade. Stir constantly until gravy thickens.

8.   Remove gravy from heat and stir in tofu cream. Add salt and pepper to taste.

9.   To serve, place the swordfish on a platter and pour the gravy over it.

Greek Smoked Eggplant

yield 2 servings

NOODLES

4 ounces very thin soba noodles

1 ounce sundried tomatoes (reconstituted if dried), drained and chopped (reserve the liquid)

1 tablespoon tomato juice with 1 teaspoon tomato paste added to thicken

1 teaspoon extra-virgin olive oil

1 tablespoon finely chopped fresh flat-leaf parsley

1 teaspoon cumin

1 clove elephant garlic, pressed, or 4 cloves regular garlic

Sea salt to taste

Freshly ground black pepper to taste

EGGPLANT

1 medium eggplant

1/2 small Spanish onion, finely chopped

1/4 teaspoon dried oregano

1/4 dried basil

1/2 tablespoon finely chopped Italian parsley

1 1/2 tablespoons extra virgin olive oil

1 teaspoon cumin

1/8 cup grated soy or rice parmesan

TO COMPLETE THE RECIPE

Olive oil spray

6 thick slices portabello mushroom from 1 or 2 mushrooms (also found presliced)

2 tablespoons grated soy or rice parmesan

1. *To prepare the noodles*: In a large saucepan of salted boiling water, add soba noodles and cook until *al dente*. Drain in a colander and rinse in cold water. Set aside.

2. Heat the sundried tomato liquid, tomato juice, and oil in a frying pan or skillet, adding 1/2 teaspoon olive oil if necessary.

3. Add parsley, cumin, sundried tomatoes, and garlic, and cook over low heat until the garlic begins to turn golden. Add salt and pepper to taste and allow mixture to cool slightly.

4. Toss sauce with pasta and set aside.

5. *To prepare the eggplant:* Blacken and blister eggplant on all sides by placing under direct heat or flame. Cool the eggplant and remove and discard the blackened skins and dark seeds. Squeeze out bitter juices.

6. Place the eggplant in food processor with onion, oregano, basil, parsley, oil, cumin, and soy parmesan. Purée until smooth, and set aside.

7. *To complete the recipe:* Preheat oven to 350°.

8. Use olive oil to grease 2 individual casserole dishes, spoon in enough noodles to cover the bottom of the dish. Push firmly into the corners.

9. Spread 1 spoonful eggplant purée over noodles, arrange 3 slices of portabello mushrooms over purée, spray with olive oil spray, and cover with remaining purée, noodles, and grated soy parmesan.

10. Cover with aluminum foil and bake 7-10 minutes. Remove from oven and serve immediately.

Greek Seafarer

yield 2 servings

Olive oil cooking spray

1 teaspoon fresh Italian parsley, divided

1 teaspoon rice vinegar

1/4 teaspoon finely grated fresh ginger, optional

1 teaspoon freshly ground cinnamon

1 teaspoon freshly ground cumin

1 tablespoon extra-virgin olive oil

1 1/2 teaspoons freshly squeezed lemon juice

2 salmon fillets

Cooked basmati rice

1/2 cup lightly steamed fresh spinach, finely chopped for garnish

Sea salt to taste

Freshly ground black pepper to taste

1.   Spray a large skillet with oil and heat over medium heat. Add 1/2 teaspoon parsley and rice vinegar, and allow to warm. Set aside.

2.   With a mortar and pestle, grind together ginger, cinnamon, and cumin until you have an original spice mélange. Add olive oil, blend well, and combine with parsley mixture in skillet. Heat skillet to medium-low, and blend well until a sauce forms. Add lemon juice to taste.

3.   Soak salmon in this mixture for 5 minutes, then sauté all ingredients for approximately 8 minutes, turning fillets over halfway through. You may place fish under the broiler for an extra 2-3 minutes if no browning appears or if fillets are very thick.

4.   Serve over rice. Salt and pepper to taste. Garnish with steamed spinach or toss rice with spinach. Garnish with remaining parsley.

Cauliflower with Shiitake Mushrooms

yield 2 servings

1/2 head cauliflower

1/4 cup chopped, cooked
shiitake mushrooms

1/4 cup grated extra firm tofu

1/2 cup egg substitute

1/2 tablespoon soy flour

1/2 teaspoon sea salt

1/2 cup soy or rice milk

1 tablespoon dry soy powder

2 tablespoons rice syrup

1 clove garlic

2 teaspoons grated lemon

Grated soy cheddar cheese
for topping

1. Break off cauliflower flowerets and cook in slightly salted water until almost tender.

2. Oil a baking dish, arrange a bottom layer of cauliflower followed by a layer of mushrooms. Top with grated tofu.

3. Preheat oven to 325°. Blend the egg substitute, flour, salt, and rice milk (enriched with extra soy powder), rice syrup, garlic, and lemon.

4. Pour mixture over layers in baking dish. Sprinkle the top with cheese and bake until sauce thickens, approximately 25 minutes.

Eggplant Goulash

yield 2 servings

1 medium eggplant, peeled and cubed

3 tablespoons tamari

2 tablespoons olive oil

1 yellow onion, coarsely chopped

1/4 cup water

1 tablespoon paprika

1/2 green bell pepper, coarsely chopped

1 tablespoon red miso paste

1 teaspoon garlic powder

Yellow and orange bell pepper slices and carrot peels for garnish

1. Toss eggplant in a bowl with tamari and olive oil. Heat a sauté pan over medium heat and brown the eggplant.

2. Remove eggplant, and in the same pan sauté the onion.

3. Deglaze the pan with water, and then add paprika, pepper, miso paste, and garlic powder. Simmer until peppers are soft, then toss with the eggplant.

4. Serve over noodles, garnished with yellow and orange pepper slices and carrot peels.

Paprika Swordfish

yield 2 servings

FISH
1 tablespoon olive oil
1 pound swordfish, cubed

SAUCE
1 tablespoon olive oil
1/2 yellow onion, finely chopped
1 tablespoon tamari
1 teaspoon paprika

1/2 cup silken tofu, processed until creamy in blender or food processor
1 tablespoon prepared mustard
1 tablespoon prepared horseradish
1 teaspoon lemon juice
1 teaspoon lime juice
Yellow, red, orange, purple, and black pepper slices for garnish

1. *To prepare the fish*: In sauté pan, heat the oil over medium heat, and cook swordfish until it is opaque and flakes when probed with a fork, about 15 minutes.

2. *To prepare the sauce*: In a saucepan, heat the oil over medium heat and brown the onion, then add tamari, paprika, tofu, mustard, horseradish, and lemon and lime juices. Heat through, then toss with the swordfish.

3. Serve with noodles and garnish with fresh pepper slices.

Sauerkraut Pockets

yield 2 servings

2 cups prepared sauerkraut

4 large, unbroken cabbage leaves

2 cups diced seitan

1 tablespoon olive oil

1 small onion, chopped

1 cup texturized vegetable protein (TVP)

$1/3$ cup cooked basmati rice

$1/4$ cup egg substitute

$1^1/2$ teaspoons sea salt

$1/4$ teaspoon paprika

1 teaspoon white pepper

Mock Sour Cream (see page 33)

1. Heat the sauerkraut in a saucepan.

2. In another pan, steam cabbage leaves until wilted. Drain the leaves and allow to cool.

3. In a sauté pan, heat the oil over medium heat and cook the seitan and onion until golden.

4. Add TVP and cook until the crumbles brown.

5. Stir in rice, egg substitute, sea salt, paprika, and pepper.

6. Divide this mixture equally, and spread on the 4 cabbage leaves. Roll up leaves and tuck in the ends.

7. Remove half the sauerkraut from the pan and set aside. Place the cabbage rolls on top of the sauerkraut left in the saucepan. Then cover cabbage rolls with the remaining sauerkraut. Simmer for 10 minutes.

8. Top with Mock Sour Cream just before serving.

Stuffed Head of Cabbage

yield 2 servings

1 head cabbage, cored

2 cups cooked brown rice

Sea salt to taste

Freshly ground black pepper
to taste

1 teaspoon minced fresh
garlic

1/8 teaspoon minced fresh
ginger

1 teaspoon sesame oil

1/4 teaspoon soy sauce

1/4 cup peas

SWEET AND SOUR SAUCE

2 teaspoons honey

1 teaspoon tamari

1 teaspoon dried mint

1/4 teaspoon dried oregano

1/4 cup firm tofu, grated

Curly parsley for garnish

1. To remove the core from the cabbage, heat boiling salted water and cook cabbage until tender. Drain water and scoop out the center.

2. Season the rice with sea salt, pepper, garlic, ginger, sesame oil, and soy sauce. Stuff rice into cabbage and add peas. Place cabbage into a deep baking dish.

3. *To prepare the sauce:* Mix together honey, tamari, mint, and oregano.

4. Preheat oven to 350°.

5. Cover cabbage with sweet and sour sauce and top with grated tofu. Bake for 20 minutes. Garnish with curly parsley.

Indian Ratatouille

yield 2 servings

1 large eggplant, cut into
  medium slices

1¹/2 teaspoons sea salt

2 tablespoons hazelnut or
  olive oil

3 tablespoons diced onion

2 cloves garlic, chopped

¹/2 teaspoon freshly grated
  ginger

2 tomatoes, sliced

1 zucchini, cut into ¹/2-inch
  slices

2 medium potatoes, cut into
  ¹/2-inch slices

1 cup cauliflower flowerets

2 red or yellow bell peppers

1 green chile pepper, finely
  chopped

¹/4 cup okra

¹/4 cup button mushrooms

1 teaspoon anise

1 teaspoon cardamom

1 teaspoon ground cloves

Watercress for garnish

1.   Sprinkle eggplant slices with 1 teaspoon sea salt and let rest
30 minutes. Rinse and pat dry.

2.   Heat oil in a saucepan over medium heat, and sauté the
onion and garlic until translucent. Add ginger and tomatoes and cook
for 3 minutes.

3.   Stir in zucchini, potatoes, cauliflower, and peppers, and mix
well. Cook 5 minutes, then add chile peppers, okra, mushrooms,
anise, cardamom, cloves, and remaining salt. Cover pan and simmer
10-15 minutes until vegetables are tender.

4.   Serve hot, garnished with watercress.

Potato Masala Curry

yield 2 servings

2 medium potatoes, cubed
1/4 cup fresh peas
2 large onions, diced
1/2 teaspoon turmeric
1 teaspoon sea salt, divided
1/4 teaspoon cayenne
3 tablespoons grated fresh or dried unsweetened coconut
1/2 teaspoon ginger powder

1 tablespoon toasted sesame oil
1/2 teaspoon mustard seeds
1 teaspoon cardamom
1 teaspoon anise seed
2 black peppercorns
1 teaspoon curry
Leaves from 1 sprig of coriander and grated carrot for garnish

1. Cook the potatoes and peas in just enough water to cover along with three-quarters of the diced onions, turmeric, 1/2 teaspoon salt, and cayenne until half-cooked, 8 minutes.

2. Purée the coconut and ginger in a blender. Add to the potatoes and cook for 8 more minutes, until tender but not soft.

3. Heat the oil in a skillet and add the mustard seeds. Allow to sizzle for a few seconds until all have popped, then add the remaining diced onions, cardamom, anise seed, and peppercorns, and fry until golden. Stir in with potatoes.

4. Add curry and remaining salt and garnish with coriander and grated carrot.

Rice and Lentils (Dahl)

yield 2 servings

2 cups basmati rice

1 cup washed red or yellow
  lentils

1 cup button mushrooms

3 cloves garlic, thinly sliced

1 yellow onion, chopped

4 cups water

1 tablespoon soy sauce

3 tablespoons toasted sesame
  oil

1 teaspoon cumin seeds

2 teaspoons sea salt

Orange wedges for garnish

1. Combine the rice, lentils, mushrooms, garlic, and onion in a large bowl. Add enough water to cover. Soak for 1 hour, then drain and rinse.

2. Place the mixture in a heavy ovenproof pan. Add the water and soy sauce. Bring to a boil over medium heat. Cover, reduce heat, and simmer for 20 minutes.

3. Preheat oven to 450°.

4. Turn the oven off and place the tightly covered pan of cooked rice and lentils in the oven. Allow to sit for 20 minutes to absorb excess moisture.

5. In a small frying pan, warm the oil over medium heat. Add the cumin seeds, and salt, and sauté until brown and fragrant.

6. Serve rice and lentils hot, topped with cumin seasoning and garnished with orange wedges around the edge of the plate.

Dijon Fish, Noodles, and Vegetables

yield 2 servings

Olive oil cooking spray

1 small yellow onion, quartered and thickly sliced

1 scallion, diced

1 small carrot, thinly sliced

1/2 small red bell pepper

1/2 small green bell pepper

1/2 small fresh Anaheim chile, seeded and finely chopped

1 1/2 teaspoons Dijon style mustard

1 clove fresh, crushed elephant garlic or 3 cloves regular garlic

1/4 teaspoon cayenne, or to taste

1/2 teaspoon soy sauce, plus additional to taste

2 teaspoons sesame, peanut, or olive oil

1/4 cup water

Sea salt

Freshly ground pepper to taste

2 mako, thrusher, or blackfin shark steaks (salmon steaks may be substituted)

Pinch cumin seed, crushed well (use mortar and pestle)

1 tablespoon ground flaxseed

5 ounces extra long Chinese noodles, cooked

Honey (optional)

1. In a large skillet sprayed with olive oil, sauté onion, scallion, carrot, peppers, Anaheim chile, mustard, garlic, and cayenne. When carrot strips are crisp-tender, add 1/4 teaspoon soy sauce, sesame oil, water, salt, and pepper to taste. Mix well and set aside.

2. Spray another large skillet with olive oil, and heat over medium heat. Place the shark steaks in the pan with crushed cumin and 1/4 teaspoon soy sauce. Brown shark lightly on both sides, leaving the inside not quite cooked, approximately 2 minutes.

3. Drain the oil and juices from the vegetable mixture into a small saucepan. Add flaxseed and heat until thickened; set aside.

4. Cover entire bottom of nonstick baking pan with vegetable mixture. Lay shark steaks on the vegetables, with thickened mixture on top. Broil for 2 minutes.

5. Place cooked noodles (tossed with pinch of salt and freshly ground pepper, if desired) in a decorative dish. Cover the center with the vegetable mixture, and top with shark steaks.

6. Serve immediately. Use remaining thickened mixture as side sauce, with a little honey added, if desired.

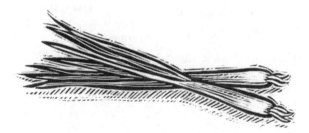

Collards and Potatoes

yield 2 servings

1 tablespoon olive oil
1 leek, chopped
1/2 small onion
1 clove elephant garlic or 3 regular cloves, chopped
2 cups chopped collard greens
1 cup chopped spinach
1 tablespoon finely chopped fresh parsley

1 bay leaf
2 russet potatoes, peeled and cubed
1 sweet potato, chopped
1/8 teaspoon powdered thyme
1/2 cup soy or rice milk powder with 1/4 cup potato water
Paprika

1. In a sauté pan, heat the oil over medium heat. Sauté the leek, onion, and garlic until soft, approximately 8-10 minutes.

2. Add collards, spinach, and parsley. Cover and cook until tender, stirring frequently, approximately 17-20 minutes.

3. In salted water with bay leaf and thyme, boil potatoes until they slide off a fork. Drain, reserving 1/4 cup cooking water.

4. Place the potato cubes in a medium bowl, and add the collards. Slowly add the reconstituted rice or soy milk until moderately thick.

5. Garnish with a sprinkle of paprika.

Cucumber Trout

yield 2 servings

1 small cucumber, sliced
    wafer-thin into rounds
1 teaspoon fresh minced
    fennel
1 teaspoon red wine vinegar
1/8 teaspoon vegetable
    bouillon
Dash of garlic powder

SAUCE
1 cup silken tofu
Zest and juice of 1 lemon
Pinch sea salt
1/2 teaspoon almond oil

1 pound brook trout, filleted
1 tablespoon roasted slivered
    almonds, as garnish

1. Preheat oven to 375°.

2. In a small bowl, combine cucumber, fennel, and red wine vinegar. Season with vegetable bouillon and a dash of garlic powder. Toss to coat.

3. *To prepare the sauce:* In a blender, combine tofu, lemon zest and juice, and a pinch of salt.

4. Line a baking sheet with parchment paper. Place trout, skins down, on the sheet. Brush with almond oil and wrap the trout in parchment, tucking the paper ends under the fish. Bake until center is no longer translucent, about 20 minutes.

5. Place a bed of cucumbers on each plate.

6. Carefully open parchment, directing the steam away from face and hands. Place trout again skin side down on top of plate.

7. Top with a generous dollop of creamy tofu sauce. Garnish with a sprinkle of roasted slivered almonds.

Mock Meatball Veggie Stew

yield 2 servings

1/4 teaspoon salt

1/8 teaspoon white pepper

Dash Tabasco sauce

1 tablespoon Worcestershire sauce

1 teaspoon grated orange peel

1/2 teaspoon dried thyme

1 tablespoon curry powder

1 teaspoon tamari

1 stalk celery, chopped

1 scallion, chopped

2 tablespoons egg substitute

1 tablespoon Bragg's liquid aminos (available in health food stores)

4 ounces textured vegetable protein (TVP)

1/4 cup spelt flour

1 tablespoon sunflower oil

1 cup yellow squash, sliced

1 small turnip, boiled and cubed

1 medium red potato, boiled, and shredded

1 cup fresh tomato, peeled, cored, and chopped

1 leek, with top, sliced

1 quart fish broth (see page 38), or vegetable bouillon

1 tablespoon chopped parsley

1.   Combine salt, pepper, Tabasco, Worcestershire, orange peel, thyme, curry, tamari, celery, scallion, egg substitute, aminos, and TVP. Shape into 1-inch balls and roll in spelt flour.

2.   Heat oil in a skillet and brown the balls, turning gently between a fork and a spoon. Set aside. Save any drippings.

3.   In a large saucepan, place the squash, turnip, potato, tomato, leek, and broth. Boil on medium heat for approximately 30 minutes.

4.   Add the meatballs to soup and reheat for 5-7 minutes. Sprinkle parsley on top. Serve with toasted homemade bread.

Spaghetti with Garlic and Oil

yield 2 servings

1/4 cup olive oil

5 cloves garlic, minced

1/4 teaspoon crushed red pepper

1/4 cup parsley, chopped

1/2 cup arugula, chopped

1/4 cup basil

2 tomatoes

3 black olives, pitted and chopped

1 tablespoon pine nuts

1/2 pound spaghetti, cooked according to package instructions

1. In a sauté pan, heat the oil over medium-high heat and add the garlic and red pepper, stirring constantly to keep from burning.

2. When the garlic starts to brown, stir in the chopped parsley, arugula, basil, tomatoes, olives, and pine nuts. When the arugula is wilted, remove the sauce from heat and toss with cooked spaghetti.

Linguine with White Tempeh Sauce

yield 2 servings

1/3 cup olive oil

1/4 teaspoon crushed red pepper

2 cloves garlic, minced

1/2 pound tempeh, cut into 3/4-inch cubes

1/2 tablespoon dried thyme

1 teaspoon sea salt

1 teaspoon lemon juice

1/8 teaspoon dill

1/2 teaspoon oregano

1/2 pound linguine, cooked according to package instructions

1.   In a large sauté pan, heat the oil, red pepper, and garlic over medium-high heat until the oil is sizzling hot, about 2 minutes.

2.   Add the tempeh, thyme, salt, lemon juice, dill, and oregano and cook 8-10 minutes. Toss with cooked linguine.

Fettuccine with Salmon

yield 2 servings

1/4 cup olive oil

3 large cloves garlic, thinly
sliced

1/4 teaspoon crushed red
pepper

1/4 cup tomatoes, chopped

1 teaspoon dried basil

1/4 cup fresh parsley,
chopped

1 tablespoon dried oregano

1/8 teaspoon white pepper

1 teaspoon tarragon

1/2 pound salmon, grilled or
broiled, cut into bite size
pieces

1 pound fettuccine, cooked
according to package
instructions

1.　In a sauté pan, heat the oil over medium-high heat. Cook the garlic and pepper until sizzling, about 2 minutes.

2.　Add the tomatoes and stir over high heat for 1 minute.

3.　Add basil, parsley, oregano, pepper, and tarragon and stir for another 2 minutes.

4.　Add the salmon, turn off the heat, and mix well.

5.　Toss with the cooked fettuccine.

Eggplant Parmigiana Elinia

yield 2 servings

2 small to medium peeled
  eggplants

Sea salt to taste

1/8 cup extra-virgin olive oil

1/2 cup tofu cream cheese
  blended with 2 sprigs
  chopped saffron

1/4 pound fresh soy moz-
  zarella, thinly sliced

1 small can tomato sauce

1 teaspoon dried oregano

1/4 teaspoon cayenne

1 tablespoon freshly chopped
  basil

1.   Cut the eggplants into 1/4-inch thick slices. Sprinkle the slices with salt, and weigh them down with a heavy plate. Let stand for 1 hour or overnight. Drain and rinse the slices and pat them dry.

2.   In a heavy skillet, heat the oil over medium-high heat. Sauté the eggplant slices until golden brown on both sides. Drain on paper towels.

3.   Preheat the oven to 350°.

4.   In a round casserole dish, layer eggplant, tofu cream cheese mixture, soy mozzarella, tomato sauce, oregano, and cayenne. Continue to build layers until you have used up all of the ingredients. The final layer should be the tofu cream cheese sprinkled with basil.

5.   Bake the eggplant for 20 minutes until the top is golden brown and bubbly.

Pesto a la Mariano

yield 2 servings

1 clove elephant garlic,
   pressed, or 4 cloves
   regular garlic
1 scallion, chopped
1/4 teaspoon sea salt
1 1/4 cups fresh basil leaves
1/2 teaspoon dried oregano
1/3 cup extra-virgin olive oil

1 ounce pine nuts or walnuts
3/4 cup soy parmesean
1/2 teaspoon lemon juice
Freshly ground black pepper
   to taste
12 ounces capellini

1.   Mix the garlic with scallion, salt, basil, and oregano, using a mortar and pestle to pound the ingredients together.

2.   Keep mixing, adding olive oil a little at a time. Slowly fold in the pine nuts, 1/4 cup of the soy parmesan, lemon juice, and black pepper. Continue mixing with mortar and pestle or transfer to food processor and pulse for 1-2 minutes or until the sauce is a chunky or pulpy consistency. Cover with olive oil and refrigerate for 30 minutes before using.

3.   Cook the capellini in plenty of lightly salted boiling water. Drain, saving a little of the cooking water to add to the pesto sauce.

4.   Toss the capellini and the pesto and a little bit of the cooking water in a large bowl, along with the remaining soy parmesan and olive oil. Sprinkle with black pepper and serve immediately.

Marsala Salmon

yield 2 servings

2 thick salmon steaks

Spelt flour for dredging and thickening sauce

1 1/3 tablespoons chopped parsley

1 1/2 tablespoons extra-virgin olive oil

Minced shallots to taste

6 large slices portabello mushrooms (also sold presliced)

3/4 cup marsala wine, wine vinegar, or nonalcoholic balsamic vinegar

1/2 teaspoon lemon pepper or freshly ground black pepper

Sea salt to taste

1. Dredge the salmon in spelt flour and 1/2 teaspoon of the parsley and lightly pound each steak for 1/2 minute.

2. Warm the olive oil in a large skillet over medium heat. Add salmon steaks and sauté on both sides until golden. Remove steaks from pan.

3. Sauté shallots and portabello mushrooms for 5 minutes.

4. Pour marsala wine into the pan to deglaze.

5. Reduce heat to low, and stir 1 tablespoon of flour into the wine. Return the salmon to the pan, turning to coat with the sauce.

6. Cover and cook over low heat for 3 minutes.

7. Season with pepper and salt to taste, sprinkle with remaining parsley, and serve hot.

Neapolitan Salmon Portabello

2 salmon steaks (or swordfish or mackerel)

1^1/$_2$ teaspoons freshly squeezed lemon juice

1 tablespoon sea salt

1 teaspoon white pepper

1 teaspoon ground allspice

1^1/$_2$ tablespoons spelt crumbs (from dried spelt bread) or spelt flour

1 small vidalia onion, chopped

^{1}/$_2$ tablespoon fresh basil, chopped

^{3}/$_8$-^{1}/$_2$ cup egg substitute

1 teaspoon dried oregano, sautéed (optional)

1^1/$_2$ tablespoons extra-virgin olive oil

^{1}/$_4$ cup white wine or sherry

14-ounce can plum tomatoes with juice

^{1}/$_2$ tablespoon fresh chopped oregano

^{1}/$_3$ cup dry red wine

8 large thick slices portabello mushrooms from 1-2 mushrooms (also sold presliced)

^{1}/$_2$ cup cooked risotto (follow instructions on package)

^{1}/$_4$ cup grated soy pecorino or soy parmesan

^{1}/$_4$ pound soy ricotta (or tofu ricotta; see Vegetarian Lasagna, page 164)

^{1}/$_2$ pound soy mozzarella, diced

1.   In a blender, blend together salmon, lemon juice, sea salt, white pepper, and allspice, and let sit.

2.   Combine salmon mixture with spelt crumbs or flour, onion, half of the basil, and egg substitute. Mix with a fork, breaking the salmon into small pieces.

3.   With your hands, form mixture into loosely packed balls approximately 1-2 inches in diameter. Roll them between your palms to make them round and firm. Roll in extra spelt crumbs or flour if not firm enough, adding sautéed oregano if extra flavor is desired. Salmon balls must be firm but not overworked.

4.   Heat the olive oil in a large skillet at medium heat, and brown salmon balls on all sides. Pour in white wine, reduce heat, and cook for 4 minutes.

5.   In another pot, simmer tomatoes, the remaining basil, oregano, and red wine for 20 minutes.

6.   Add the sauce to salmon balls and cook over medium heat for an additional 3 minutes. Take salmon balls out and set aside.

7.   In another pan over medium heat, sauté portabello mushrooms in olive oil on both sides until they start to turn light brown. Set aside.

8.   Toss cooked risotto with $1/2$ tablespoon soy pecorino (or soy parmesan), and 2 tablespoons of the tomato sauce.

9.   Preheat oven to 350°.

10.   In an ovenproof casserole dish, layer one-third of the sauce, one-half of the ricotta, one-half of the salmon balls, one-third of the soy pecorino, and a layer of portabello mushrooms. Repeat the layering, and finish with a layer of soy mozzarella and any remaining soy cheeses.

11.   Bake in oven for 12-18 minutes or until the top is light golden brown.

Northern Italian Baked Ziti with Portabello

yield 2 servings

1/2 pound salmon or mackerel soaked in white wine for 1 1/2 hours

1/4 cup egg substitute

1 tablespoon dry whole-grain bread crumbs

1/2 onion, chopped (vidalia if milder taste is preferred)

1 1/2 tablespoons extra-virgin olive oil

1 1/2 cup fresh tomatoes, chopped

1/4-1/2 tablespoon fresh basil, chopped

1/2 pound ziti

1/4 cup freshly grated soy pecorino or soy parmesan or tofu soaked in fat free Italian dressing

8 large slices Portabello cut from 1-2 mushrooms (also sold presliced)

1/4 pound soy ricotta or tofu ricotta (see Vegetarian Lasagna, page 164)

1/4 pound soy mozzarella, diced

1.   Make salmon balls by mashing the salmon, egg substitute, bread crumbs, and onion with a fork. Pack tightly with your fingers to form into balls about 2 inches in diameter. Roll them between palms until round and firm.

2.   Heat half the oil in a medium skillet over medium-high heat, and brown the salmon balls on all sides. Reduce heat to low, and cook for 5 minutes. Remove from pan and set aside.

3.   Add tomatoes and basil to pan, and simmer for 15 minutes.

4.   Meanwhile, cook the ziti in a large pot of salted, boiling water until still a bit hard to the bite. Drain and toss with 1/2 tablespoon soy pecorino or soy parmesan and 2 tablespoons of the sauce.

5. In a sauté pan, heat remaining oil over medium heat, and sauté the portabello slices 1 minute on each side. Set aside.

6. Preheat the oven to 425°.

7. In an ovenproof casserole, layer one-third of the remaining sauce, the pasta, one-half of the soy ricotta, one-third of the soy mozzarella, one-half the salmon balls, and one-third soy pecorino or soy parmesan. Continue layering until all ingredients are used up.

8. Bake for 20 minutes or until light golden.

Vegetarian Lasagna

yield 2 servings

PASTA

1/2 tablespoon salt

4 tablespoons olive oil

1/2 pound dried spinach
lasagna

TOFU RICOTTA

1 package tofu

1 tablespoon tahini

1 1/2 teaspoons umeboshi
plum paste

TO COMPLETE THE RECIPE

1 eggplant, peeled and cut
lengthwise into 1/4-inch
slices

1 zucchini, cut lengthwise
into 1/4-inch slices

1/2 pound fresh shiitake
mushrooms, sliced

1/2 pound tempeh, cut into
chunks

4 cups fresh arugula

1 tablespoon dried bread
crumbs

2 cloves garlic, chopped

1/2 tablespoon parsley,
chopped

1/4 teaspoon salt

1/2 teaspoon freshly ground
black pepper

1 1/2 cups tomato sauce

3/4 cup tofu ricotta (soy
ricotta may also be found
at health food stores)

3/4 cup soy parmesan

1. *To prepare the pasta*: Add salt and 1 tablespoon of oil to a large pot of boiling water. Add the pasta pieces one by one and cook for 8-10 minutes.

2. Carefully remove the pasta and pat dry.

3. *To prepare the tofu*: Mix tofu ricotta ingredients in a small bowl.

4. *To complete the recipe*: In a large saucepan, heat the remaining oil over medium heat, and sauté the eggplant, zucchini, mushrooms, tempeh, arugula, bread crumbs, garlic, parsley, salt, and pepper for 10 minutes.

5. Preheat oven to 375°.

6. Put 3-4 tablespoons tomato sauce on the bottom of a large baking dish. Cover with a layer of pasta. Add a layer of the vegetable mixture, then a layer of the ricotta mixture, and then the soy parmesan, and then 3-4 tablespoons tomato sauce.

7. Starting with the tomato sauce, repeat the sequence of layers until the ingredients are all used.

8. Bake for 20 minutes, and serve hot.

Tempeh Cacciatora Sauce

yield 2 servings

1¹/₂ cups shiitake mush-
rooms, sliced (fresh, or
dried and reconstituted;
see step 1)

¹/₈ cup olive oil

1 tablespoon macadamia or
olive oil

2 cups tempeh, cut into
chunks

3 cloves garlic, minced

1 medium white onion,
chopped

2 cups plum tomatoes with
juice

1 large green pepper, sliced
thin

1 large red pepper, sliced
thin

1 large yellow pepper, sliced
thin

¹/₈ cup chopped fresh
parsley

¹/₂ cup chopped arugula

¹/₂ teaspoon dried oregano

¹/₂ teaspoon dried thyme

2 bay leaves

¹/₃ cup dry red wine

¹/₂ teaspoon sea salt

¹/₂ teaspoon black pepper

Spaghetti, cooked

1. *To reconstitute mushrooms:* Place dried mushrooms in a saucepan and cover with water. Bring to a rolling boil, then reduce heat and simmer 20 minutes. Drain and slice.

2. In a large skillet, heat the oil over medium heat and sauté the tempeh, garlic, and onion for 5 minutes. Add the mushrooms and sauté for 5 minutes more.

3. Add the tomatoes, peppers, parsley, arugula, oregano, thyme, bay leaves, wine, salt, and pepper and simmer for 25-30 minutes.

4. Serve over cooked spaghetti.

Almost Locrio Stew

yield 2 servings

$^1/4$ cup sundried tomatoes

$^1/3$ cup water

2 scallions, with tops, chopped

1 cup chopped onion (preferably Bermuda)

1 green pepper, diced

8 ounces Morning Star breakfast vegetable links, sliced

$^1/4$ cup canola oil

$^1/2$ teaspoon sea salt

2 plum tomatoes, chopped

$^1/4$ teaspoon crushed whole or ground cloves

$^1/4$ teaspoon annatto

1 tablespoon dried or fresh chives

1 habañero pepper, whole

2 cloves garlic, minced

8 ounces calabaza, peeled and diced

Cooked white basmati rice

Parsley sprigs for garnish

1. Purée sundried tomatoes and $^1/3$ cup water in blender, and set aside.

2. In a stockpot, sauté the scallions, onion, green pepper, and sausage slices in the canola oil. Add sundried tomato paste, salt, chopped plum tomatoes, cloves, annatto, chives, pepper, garlic, and diced calabaza. Cover with ample water. Cover and simmer approximately 1 hour.

3. Serve with cooked white basmati rice. Garnish with fresh chopped parsley.

Disappearing Codfish

yield 2 servings

MANGO MAYONNAISE
1/2 cup fresh mango

1 cup safflower mayonnaise (available at health food stores)

1/2 teaspoon Dijon mustard

1 teaspoon fresh squeezed lemon juice

1 teaspoon honey

FISH
1/2 pound salted codfish

2 scallions, finely chopped

1 fresh hot pepper, seeded

1 clove garlic, crushed

1 tablespoon chopped parsley

1/4 teaspoon ground allspice

BATTER
2 cups whole wheat pastry flour

2 1/2 teaspoons baking powder

1 teaspoon annatto oil or olive oil

1/4 cup egg substitute

1/4 cup coconut milk

TO COMPLETE THE RECIPE
Macadamia or canola oil

Curly parsley for garnish

1. *To prepare the mayonnaise*: Blend or purée all mango mayonnaise ingredients.

2. *To prepare the fish*: Soak the codfish in cold water for about 15 minutes (depending on the hardness of the fish). Drain and remove any bones and skin. Flake the codfish flesh into a large bowl with scallions, hot pepper, garlic, parsley, and allspice.

3. *To prepare the batter*: Sift the flour with baking powder into a bowl. Add annatto oil, egg substitute, and coconut milk. Beat the mixture to combine well.

4. Stir codfish-spice mixture into batter. Allow to stand for 10 minutes.

5. *To complete the recipe*: In a heavy cast iron pot, heat macadamia oil over medium heat. Drop fish by spoonfuls, a few at a time, into oil. Fry until golden brown. Drain on paper towels, garnish with parsley, and serve with mango mayonnaise.

Tamarindo Jerked Sturgeon

yield 2 servings

MANGO CHUTNEY

2 ripe mangoes, peeled and mashed

8 figs, mashed into a paste

2 sprigs fresh parsley, chopped

1/4 cup honey

1/4 teaspoon cayenne

1/4 teaspoon sea salt

TO COMPLETE THE RECIPE

1 teaspoon ground allspice

1 tablespoon ground cardamom

1/2 teaspoon ground cinnamon

1/2 teaspoon sea salt

1/2 cup diced white onion

2 cloves garlic, diced

2 tablespoons toasted sesame oil

1/4 teaspoon ground nutmeg

1/4 teaspoon cayenne

1/4 teaspoon freshly ground black pepper

1 tablespoon hot pepper sauce (such as Tobasco)

1 tablespoon honey (orange blossom preferred)

1/2 pound sturgeon cut into 1-inch pieces

1. *To prepare the chutney:* In a food processor or blender, combine the chutney ingredients and blend into a paste. Refrigerate until ready to serve.

2. *To complete the recipe*: Mix together all ingredients except the sturgeon, and stir-fry 10 minutes over medium heat.

3. Broil fish for 8 minutes on each side, then cut into pieces and add to stir fry.

4. Serve warm with mango chutney.

Jerked Fish

y i e l d   2   s e r v i n g s

20 allspice berries

12 coriander seeds

2 cinnamon sticks

1 teaspoon freshly grated
  nutmeg

4 scallions, with tops, sliced

1 tablespoon red pepper
  flakes

1 teaspoon kosher salt or sea
  salt

1 teaspoon freshly ground
  black pepper

1 tablespoon puréed ginger

1/4 cup olive oil

1 tablespoon rum

1/8 cup date sugar or raw
  sugar

1 pound marion fish or
  swordfish

Lime slices and hot sauce for
  garnish

Mustard sauce (optional)

1. Roast allspice and coriander gently in a nonstick pan, stirring constantly, 1-2 minutes, or until they begin to brown.

2. Put roasted spices and all remaining ingredients, except the fish, into a blender or coffee mill and grind into a paste.

3. Rub the paste all over the fish. Place fish in ziptop bag(s), squeezing all the air out. Marinate in refrigerator overnight.

4. Grill or pan fry for 15 minutes.

5. Serve over brown rice with peas. Garnish with slice of lime and hot sauce. Serve with a mustard sauce.

Codfish and Ackee

1 ounce ackee

3/4 pound codfish fillet

2 tablespoons coconut or canola oil

1/2 red bell pepper

2 scallions, finely chopped

2 medium tomatoes, seeded and chopped

1 teaspoon Bragg's liquid aminos

1/4 teaspoon freshly ground black pepper

1/4 Scotch Bonnet pepper, seeded and finely chopped

1/4 teaspoon sea salt

1 teaspoon chopped thyme leaves or 1/4 teaspoon dried

1 tablespoon lemon juice

1 lemon cut into wedges

Watercress sprigs for garnish

Rice, cooked (optional)

1. Drain liquid from can of ackee. (If using fresh ackee, remove all seeds and membranes and boil in lightly salted water approximately 20 minutes. Drain and keep warm.)

2. Poach codfish in water for 15-20 minutes. Remove from water and cool. Flake the flesh with a fork when cool enough to handle.

3. In coconut oil, sauté red pepper, scallions, tomatoes, aminos, black pepper, Scotch Bonnet, salt, and thyme.

4. Add the codfish and stir gently. Add ackee and toss gently.

5. Spritz with a little lemon juice and garnish with lemon wedges and watercress. Serve with rice.

Curried Halibut

yield 2 servings

1 tablespoon coconut or
   canola oil

1 pound halibut fillet, cut
   into 1-inch cubes

4 scallions, chopped

2 cloves garlic, minced

1/4 teaspoon ground allspice

1 tablespoon curry powder

1 dash cayenne

1/4 teaspoon sea salt

1/8 teaspoon freshly ground
   black pepper

1/2 cup unsweetened coconut
   milk

1 teaspoon arrowroot

White basmati rice, cooked
   (optional)

Mango Chutney (optional,
   see page 170)

1.   Heat the oil in a skillet over medium heat, and brown the
halibut, scallions, and garlic until evenly cooked.

2.   Stir in allspice, curry powder, cayenne, salt, and pepper. Add
the coconut milk and arrowroot. Stir and cover. Reduce heat to low,
and simmer for 20 minutes.

3.   Serve over white basmati rice topped with mango chutney.

Jamaican Run Down

yield 2 servings

1/4 cup fresh lime juice

1 pound mackerel fillets

2 cups coconut milk (or one 8-ounce can coconut cream and 1 cup of water)

3 scallions, with tops, finely chopped

1 small Bermuda onion, chopped

2 cloves garlic, finely minced

1/2 teaspoon mustard seed

1/8 cup toasted almonds

2 medium tomatoes, peeled and chopped

1 1/2 teaspoon apple cider vinegar

1/4 teaspoon dried thyme leaves

1/8 teaspoon ground coriander

1 tablespoon fresh red hot pepper

Green Plantain Balls (page 223)

Lemon slices for garnish

1. Pour lime juice over the fish and set aside for 1/2 hour.

2. Bring a large pot of water to a boil. Remove the mackerel from the lime juice and add to the pot. Boil for 2-3 minutes. Remove and drain.

3. Gently simmer the coconut milk in a nonstick pan until it is oily. Add scallions, onion, garlic, mustard seed, almonds, and tomatoes. Stir in vinegar, thyme, coriander, and red pepper. Simmer 2-3 minutes.

4. Add fish to sauce and cook an additional 10 minutes.

5. Serve hot with Green Plantain Balls. Garnish with lemon slices.

Turned Down Cornmeal

yield 2 servings

2 tablespoons plus 1/8 cup canola oil

1 onion, minced

1 clove elephant garlic, chopped, or 4 regular cloves, crushed

Leaves of 1 thyme sprig

1 scallion, green and white parts, finely chopped

3 fresh okras sliced into rings

1/2 cup fresh or frozen corn kernels

1 plum tomato, diced

1 small sweet yellow bell pepper, diced

1 tablespoon tamari

1/2 teaspoon hot pepper sauce (Pick-A-Pepper or Tabasco)

1/4 cup diced sea bass

1 tablespoon cayenne

1 teaspoon of white pepper

1 teaspoon curry powder

1 teaspoon sea salt

2 cups soy milk

1 cup coconut milk

1 cup cornmeal

1.	Heat 2 tablespoons oil over medium heat and sauté onion, garlic, thyme, scallion, okra, corn, tomato, and yellow pepper for 5 minutes. Add tamari and hot pepper sauce.

2.	Stir in the sea bass and remaining canola oil. Season with cayenne, white pepper, curry, and sea salt. Add the soy milk to the mixture.

3.	Pour coconut milk into a double boiler. Boil until a light film appears on the surface, about 10 minutes.

4.	Add cornmeal to the fish mixture, stir well, and cover the pot. Continue cooking about 1/2 hour, stirring or turning occasionally. At the end of this process, add the coconut milk.

5.	Firmly turn the cornmeal mixture into an ovenproof glass dish or cast iron Dutch oven. Cover the dish and allow 30 minutes or more to mold. Unmold and serve hot.

Mexican Spicy Burritos

yield 2 servings

1 fresh jalapeño, minced	4 medium-size flour tortillas
4 cloves garlic, diced	1 teaspoon olive oil
1 tablespoon tamari	1 onion, thinly sliced
1 teaspoon honey	Salsa (optional)
1 pound firm tofu, cut into thin strips	

1. In a bowl, combine jalapeño, garlic, tamari, and honey. Add tofu and marinate 20 minutes.

2. Preheat oven to 350°.

3. Stack the tortillas, wrap them in a slightly damp towel, and heat in oven for 5-10 minutes.

4. In a small skillet, heat the oil over medium-high heat. Stir-fry the onion until translucent. Add tofu with its marinade, stir well to combine, and cook for 5 minutes more.

5. Spoon mixture into tortillas, roll, and serve with salsa.

Burrito with Refried Beans and Chili

yield 2 servings

1 cup refried beans

1/4 cup salsa

2 strips of your favorite chile pepper

3 tablespoons chopped onion

2 tablespoons grated soy parmesan cheese

2 tablespoons freshly ground black pepper

1 teaspoon diced garlic

3 tablespoons ground coriander

4 medium-size corn or whole wheat tortillas

1. Combine all the ingredients except the tortillas in a bowl and mix well.

2. Preheat oven to 350°.

3. Stack the tortillas, wrap them in a slightly damp towel, and heat in oven for 5-10 minutes.

4. Spread one-quarter of the filling over one half of each tortilla and roll up. Serve immediately.

Vegetarian Chili

yield 2 servings

1/2 cup toasted sesame seed oil

2 cups extra firm tofu, cut in 1/2-inch cubes

1 cup tempeh, cut in 1/2-inch cubes

1/2 cup yellow onions, chopped

1 chile pepper, chopped

1/2 tablespoon Mexican or regular oregano

1/2 tablespoon paprika

1/2 tablespoon dill

1/2 tablespoon cumin seed

1/2 tablespoon chili powder

1/2 tablespoon minced jalapeño chile

1/4 cup canola oil

2 tablespoons masa farina or whole wheat flour

2 cups cooked pinto beans

Leaves of 1 thyme sprig

1 scallion, with top, finely chopped

3 fresh okra pods sliced into rings

1/2 cup fresh or frozen corn kernels

1 plum tomato, diced

1 small sweet yellow bell pepper, diced

1 tablespoon tamari

1/2 teaspoon hot pepper sauce (Pick-A-Pepper or Tabasco)

1/4 cup diced sea bass

1 tablespoon cayenne

1 teaspoon white pepper

1 teaspoon curry powder

1 teaspoon sea salt

2 cups soy milk

1 cup tomato sauce

1/4 cup black pitted olives, sliced, and chopped tomatoes for garnish

1. In a large saucepan, heat the oil over medium heat. Add the tofu and tempeh and sauté for 2-3 minutes.

2. Add onions, chile pepper, oregano, paprika, dill, cumin seed, and chili power, and sauté until onions are translucent.

3. Add the remaining ingredients except garnish and simmer for 25-30 minutes, stirring occasionally.

4. Garnish with olives and chopped tomatoes. Serve hot.

Veracruz-style Red Snapper

1 pound cod fillets

1 rib of fresh crispy celery (or more to taste)

$1/2$ small Spanish onion, washed and quartered

$1/2$ small vidalia onion, washed and quartered

2 bay leaves

1 carrot

2 sprigs fresh parsley

1 small fresh sprig marjoram

1 small fresh sprig thyme

3 cups water

1 teaspoon fresh-squeezed lemon juice

1 teaspoon honey (optional)

$1/8$-$1/4$ cup ground flaxseed

$1 1/2$ pounds red snapper fillets, or young shark or halibut

2 cups cooked Spanish rice

$1/2$ cup fresh basil leaves

12 black olives, whole, pitted

1.   Place all ingredients except the snapper, flaxseed, and rice, in a large saucepan and bring to a boil. Reduce heat and simmer, covered, for 1 hour.

2.   Strain the liquid with a fine strainer, filling a bowl with the broth. Put solids aside to cool.

3.   Thicken the broth slowly, using the ground flaxseed. Pick out some of the fish pieces, onion, celery, and carrot pieces and place in the broth.

4.   Dip red snapper in broth and grill, being careful not to overcook, approximately 3-5 minutes each side depending on thickness.

5.   Arrange decorative dish with rice and whole pieces of vegetables. Place the small fish (cod) pieces into sauce. Stir.

6.   Place snapper on arranged plate of rice and garnish with fresh basil and black olives. Serve with broth on the side or poured over snapper.

Curried Salmon

yield 2 servings

1 tablespoon avocado or olive oil

1 medium Bermuda red onion, chopped

1 clove elephant garlic, minced, or 4 regular cloves

1/2 teaspoon minced fresh ginger

1/2 teaspoon ground turmeric

1/4 teaspoon ground coriander

3/4 teaspoon ground cumin

1 teaspoon dried basil

1 teaspoon dill

1 teaspoon whole black peppercorns

1 large potato, peeled and cubed

4 ounces unsweetened coconut milk

4 ounces soft silken tofu, mashed well

3/4 pound fresh salmon fillet

1 tablespoon lemon juice

Sea salt to taste

Exotic Rice (optional; see page 181)

1.　In a large lidded fry pan, heat the oil over medium heat. Sauté the onion for 5 minutes or until translucent. Add garlic, ginger, turmeric, coriander, cumin, basil, dill, and peppercorns. Cook on low heat for 2 minutes.

2.　Add potato and coconut milk. Bring to a boil, lower heat, and simmer about 15 minutes, covered, until potato is tender.

3.　Add tofu and salmon to the pan and gently cook until salmon is just done—when it becomes opaque and flakes when gently probed with a fork. Do not overcook.

4.　Season with lemon juice and salt, and serve with Exotic Rice.

Exotic Rice

yield 2 servings

1^1/2 tablespoons sesame oil

1 medium onion (preferably vidalia), chopped

1 small clove garlic, minced

^{1}/2-inch cinnamon stick or ^{1}/4 teaspoon ground cinnamon

2 whole cloves

^{1}/2 teaspoon sea salt

^{1}/4 teaspoon ground ginger

1 cup jasmine basmati rice, rinsed once and soaked for 5 minutes

1^3/4 cups boiling water

^{1}/4 teaspoon ground turmeric

^{1}/4 cup coconut milk

^{1}/4 cup roasted cashews and pecans

1 tablespoon fennel seed

1.   In a large saucepan, heat the sesame oil over low heat. Add the onion and garlic and cook until soft, about 10 minutes. Add the cinnamon, cloves, sea salt, and ginger.

2.   Drain the rice and add it to the pan. Toss lightly to coat with the oil.

3.   Measure 1^3/4 cups of boiling water into the rice mix. Bring to a full boil.

4.   Add the turmeric, coconut milk, nuts, and fennel seed. Reduce the heat and simmer, covered, for 15 minutes.

5.   Remove from heat and leave covered for 5-10 more minutes before serving.

Corn Pie

yield 2 servings

FILLING

1 tablespoon olive oil

1 cup chopped shiitake mushrooms

1/2 cup chopped yellow onion

2 cloves garlic, minced

DOUGH

Kernels from 2 ears of fresh corn, grated

3 tablespoons olive oil

1/4 teaspoon sea salt

1/2 teaspoon honey

1 cup yellow or white hominy, ground (or substitute frozen peas)

GARNISH

1 hard-boiled egg, sliced

5 olives, chopped

Red, yellow, purple, and green bell pepper slices for garnish

Cherry tomato for garnish.

1.   *To prepare the filling*: In a large skillet, heat the olive oil over medium heat. Add the mushrooms, onion, and garlic, and cook until onion is translucent, about 10 minutes. Set aside to cool.

2.   *To prepare the dough*: In a large bowl, combine the corn, olive oil, salt, and honey. In a skillet over low heat, cook the mixture until thickened. Add ground hominy, cook a few more minutes and set aside to cool.

3.   Preheat oven to 375°. Oil a shallow baking dish and fill with one half of the dough mixture.

4.   Add all the filling, and arrange sliced egg and olives on top. Cover with the remaining dough, smoothing out the surface. Brush with olive oil.

5.   Bake for 45 minutes or until golden brown.

6.   Garnish with red, yellow, purple, and green pepper slices and cherry tomatoes, and serve.

Salmon

yield 2 servings

MARINADE
Juice of $1/2$ lime
1 teaspoon ground ginger
1 tablespoon soy sauce
Sea salt to taste

TO COMPLETE THE RECIPE
1 pound salmon, skin on,
    boned and cubed
$1/2$ cup spelt flour
$1/4$ teaspoon paprika
Freshly ground black pepper
3 tablespoons peanut oil
Lemon slices for garnish

1. *To prepare the marinade*: In a small bowl, thoroughly mix the lime juice, ginger, soy sauce, and sea salt. Marinate salmon cubes in this mixture for 1 hour.

2. *To complete the recipe*: In a heavy cast iron skillet, heat the oil to 325°.

3. Remove salmon cubes from marinade, drain, and set aside.

4. In a small bowl, combine the flour, paprika, and pepper. Dredge the salmon cubes in the mixture.

5. Fry the salmon cubes, a few at a time to maintain proper heat of oil, until golden brown.

6. Garnish with lemon slices and serve.

Spanish Rice with Fish, Tofu, and "No-Meatballs"

yield 2 servings

RICE

2 tablespoons olive oil

1/4 cup chopped onion

1/2 red bell pepper, diced

2 cloves garlic, minced

2 cups water

2 tablespoons dry white wine

3/4 cup white jasmine basmati rice

1 small chopped tomato

1 tablespoon minced parsley

2 scallions, with tops, sliced

1 tablespoon tamari

Pinch powdered saffron

FISH

1/2 pound salmon with skin

4 smelts

Canola oil for sautéing

2 tablespoons ginger

3 tablespoons balsamic vinegar

3 tablespoons olive oil

Asparagus tips, cooked crisp-tender, roasted red pepper strips, black olives, blanched green peas for garnish

TOFU

1 clove crushed garlic

1 tablespoon tamari

1 tablespoon olive oil

1/2 pound tofu

MUSHROOM-LENTIL "NO MEAT BALLS"

1/2 cup minced shiitake mushrooms

1/4 cup minced onion

1 clove minced garlic

1 teaspoon olive oil

1 tablespoon tamari

1/2 cup cooked lentils

Pinch black pepper

Pinch nutmeg

Pinch caraway seed

1/2 cup egg substitute

1/2 cup spelt flour

1. *To prepare the rice:* In a large saucepan, heat the olive oil over medium heat. Sauté onion, red pepper, and garlic until golden. Add remaining ingredients and simmer until liquid is absorbed.

2. *To prepare the fish:* Sauté fish in oil until brown. Blend in ginger, balsamic vinegar, and olive oil. Garnish with asparagus tips, red pepper strips, olives, and peas.

3. *To prepare the tofu:* Mix together garlic, tamari, and olive oil. Marinate tofu for 1 hour in this mixture. Sear each side of marinated tofu over high heat until quite brown. Cut into thin strips.

4. *To prepare the "no meatballs":* Sauté mushrooms, onion, and garlic in olive oil. Add tamari, lentils, pepper, nutmeg, and caraway, and then remove from heat. Add the egg substitute in order to bind mixture. Form mixture into small balls, dredge in flour, and sauté until browned.

5. Arrange fish, tofu, and "no meatballs"(in any combination) on top of rice. Heat for 5 minutes and serve.

Rice with Tempeh

yield 2 servings

2 cloves garlic, chopped

1 tablespoon finely chopped parsley

3 teaspoons lemon juice

1/4 cup olive oil

Pinch ground saffron

1 teaspoon oregano

Sea salt to taste

1/2 pound tempeh or seitan cut into serving pieces

1 medium onion, chopped (vidalia preferred)

1 green bell pepper, chopped

1 red bell pepper, chopped

2 medium ripe tomatoes, peeled and chopped

1 cup long grain rice

Cumin, paprika, chili powder, freshly ground black pepper, celery seed, basil, marjoram, cayenne, and dill to taste

2 cups water

1 teaspoon honey

2 teaspoons mustard

Dash of balsamic vinegar

1.   In a mortar, crush the garlic and parsley. Mix with lemon juice, 1 tablespoon olive oil, saffron, oregano, and salt. Coat the tempeh with this mixture and let stand for 30 minutes.

2.   In a large saucepan, heat the remaining oil over medium heat, and brown the tempeh. Remove the tempeh from the pan.

3.   Sauté onion and peppers in the pan until soft. Stir in tomatoes.

4.   Add the rice and mix well to coat with oil. Stir in the seasonings to taste, add the water, and stir.

5.   Return the tempeh to the pan. Cover and simmer gently for 20 minutes until the water has been absorbed.

6.   Separately, combine the honey, mustard, and balsamic vinegar. Drizzle over tempeh before serving.

Spanish Potato Omelet

yield 2 servings

3 tablespoons canola oil, divided

2 medium potatoes, peeled and diced

Sea salt to taste

4 tablespoons chopped onion

2 organic eggs or $1/2$ cup egg substitute

Cayenne to taste

White pepper to taste

1. In a medium frying pan, heat 1 tablespoon oil over medium heat, add the potatoes and salt, and cook for 5 minutes.

2. Add the onions and continue cooking until the potatoes are soft, but not brown. Remove the potatoes and onions from the oil and drain.

3. In a separate bowl, beat the eggs, and stir in the potatoes and onions. Season to taste.

4. In a frying pan, heat 2 tablespoons oil. Pour in the egg and potato mixture, and spread evenly in pan.

5. Cook over medium heat for 2-3 minutes, shaking the pan occasionally. When the bottom of the omelet is firm, flip the omelet over and cook until golden brown.

Tempeh in Sherry Sauce

yield 2 servings

3 tablespoons canola oil

1 pound tempeh or seitan, cut in chunks

1 medium yellow onion, diced

3 cloves garlic, chopped

2 teaspoons whole wheat flour

1/4 cup vegetable broth

1 bay leaf

1 tablespoon chopped parsley

1/4 cup dry sherry

Sea salt to taste

Freshly ground black pepper to taste

Rice, cooked (optional)

1. In a large frying pan, heat the oil over medium heat. Sauté the tempeh for 2-3 minutes on both sides, and remove from the pan.

2. Sauté the onion and garlic in the oil until the onion is translucent.

3. Stir in the flour, then add the vegetable broth and mix well.

4. Add the bay leaf, parsley, sherry, and salt and pepper to taste, and simmer for 3-4 minutes. Add the tempeh, and cover and cook over low heat for 3-4 minutes.

5. Serve over rice.

Sizzling Shrimp

y i e l d   2   s e r v i n g s

1/2 pound shrimp

2 teaspoons tamarind sauce

4 teaspoons fresh-squeezed
  lime juice, divided

1 tablespoon fish sauce

2 teaspoons toasted sesame
  oil

2 cloves garlic, minced

1 small onion, finely chopped

1/2 teaspoon chopped fresh
  red chile peppers

4 kaffir lime leaves, divided

1/4 teaspoon red curry

2 teaspoons fresh lemongrass,
  chopped

1 cup coconut milk

1/4 teaspoon ground cinnamon

2 bay leaves

2 teaspoons molasses

2 teaspoons apple cider
  vinegar

1/2 cup chunky almond or
  peanut butter

1/2 cup chopped cabbage

2 cups cooked white or
  brown basmati rice

8-10 cherry tomatoes for
  garnish

1/8 teaspoon fennel seed for
  garnish

1.   Marinate prawns in tamarind sauce, half of the lime juice, and fish sauce overnight. Save drippings to add to recipe. Drain shrimp and set aside.

2.   Heat oil in nonstick skillet over medium heat, and sauté garlic, onion, chile peppers, lime leaves, curry powder and lemongrass for 2 minutes. Stir in coconut milk, cinnamon, bay leaves, marinade, molasses, the remaining lime juice, cider vinegar, and almond butter. Blend well. Reduce to a low simmer, stirring frequently until sauce thickens, approximately 20 minutes.

3.   Grill shrimp for about 10 minutes on bamboo skewers, being careful not to overcook. If you don't have a grill or it's not outdoor cooking season, then stir-fry at high heat for 15 minutes.

4.   Serve shrimp on skewers over chopped cabbage and rice. Garnish with cherry tomatoes, top with sauce, and sprinkle with fennel seed.

Minted Pine Nut Curry

yield 2 servings

1/3 cup coconut cream

1/8 cup curry paste

1 teaspoon paprika

1/2 cup coconut milk

1 teaspoon garlic oil or olive oil

4 tablespoons fresh mint, or 1 teaspoon dried

1 1/3 cups vegetable broth or bouillon

2 shallots, thinly sliced

1/4 cup honey, divided (sunflower preferred)

4 whole cardamom pods, roasted

2 bay leaves, crushed and roasted

1/2 teaspoon sea salt

1 tablespoon tamarind pulp soaked in 1 tablespoon hot water

1 small sweet potato, cubed

1 tablespoon fish sauce

1 tablespoon Bragg's liquid aminos

1/4 cup roasted pine nuts, ground

3/4 cup roasted pine nuts, whole

White basmati rice, cooked

1. In a wok over medium heat, bring coconut cream to a boil, stirring constantly while adding curry paste, for 2 minutes.

2. Add paprika, 1/8 cup coconut milk, oil, and mint, and cook 2 minutes more. Add remaining coconut milk, 1/3 cup vegetable broth, and shallots, and bring to a full boil.

3. Add 1 tablespoon honey, cardamom, bay leaves, and salt.

4. Strain tamarind juice from pulp, set aside pulp. Add tamarind juice to wok, stir and heat 2 minutes.

5. Cover cubed sweet potato with boiling water in medium saucepan and simmer until tender. Drain liquid and set aside.

6. To wok mixture, add remaining honey, fish sauce, reserved tamarind pulp, aminos, and cooked sweet potato. Heat mixture, covered, on low for 10 minutes.

7. Stir in ground and whole roasted pine nuts just before serving. Serve with rice.

Mock Meatballs in Peanut Sauce

yield 2 servings

¹/₂ cup egg substitute

¹/₄ cup oatmeal flakes

¹/₂ cup spelt flour, and additional for coating meatballs

1 teaspoon Worcestershire sauce

1 teaspoon Bragg's liquid aminos

¹/₂ pound textured vegetable protein (TVP), or ¹/₂ pound seitan

2 tablespoons peanut oil

2 cloves garlic, chopped

1 tablespoon red curry paste

¹/₈ teaspoon marjoram

¹/₂ cup thick coconut milk

1 tablespoon chunky peanut butter

2 teaspoons honey (crystallized, if available)

1 teaspoon fresh cilantro, chopped

1 scallion, with top, chopped

1. In a medium bowl, mix together egg substitute, oatmeal flakes, spelt flour, Worcestershire sauce, aminos, and TVP.

2. Shape the mixture into 1-inch balls. (Add water if too dry.) Roll balls in additional flour.

3. Heat the oil in a wok over high heat and stir-fry garlic for 1 minute. Remove garlic and set aside.

4. Reheat the oil and cook the mock meatballs in small batches (to maintain wok temperature), rotating them until all sides are brown. Remove from wok and drain on paper towels.

5. Add the red curry paste to the wok and cook for about 2 minutes, stirring continuously. Add marjoram, thick coconut milk, and peanut butter. Whisk or stir until smooth. Season with crystallized honey.

6. Immerse the meatballs in the curry sauce and simmer on low for 10 minutes.

7. Serve in a deep bowl topped with chopped cilantro and scallion.

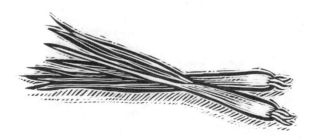

Noodles Deluxe

2 teaspoons tamarind pulp, soaked in 2 tablespoons hot water

1 cup sunflower oil

3 ounces thin rice noodles

1 clove garlic, minced

1/3 cup chopped yellow onion

1/2 cup egg substitute

8 jumbo shrimp, shelled and deveined

1/2 pound extra-firm tofu sliced 1/4-inch thick

2 teaspoons arrowroot powder

2 teaspoons fish sauce

1 tablespoon honey (tupelo preferred)

1/4 teaspoon cumin

1/4 teaspoon marjoram

1 teaspoon grated lemon zest

1 tablespoon canned yellow bean sauce

1 pickled garlic clove, sliced thinly

2 teaspoons chopped, fresh parsley; mung bean sprouts, fresh diced red chile peppers; slivered orange rind for garnish

1. Strain and discard tamarind pulp, reserving the juice.

2. Preheat oil in wok over high heat. Working a small handful at a time, fry noodles for approximately 30 seconds, turning frequently with spatula to ensure uniform cooking.

3. Remove noodles with a slotted spoon before they turn brown, and drain. Strain and reserve hot oil from wok.

4. Return 2 tablespoons of oil to wok and heat on medium until hot. Stir-fry garlic for 1 minute, then remove and set aside. Repeat with onion, and then add to garlic.

5. Cook egg substitute in wok until scrambled and golden brown. Remove and add to garlic.

6. Stir-fry shrimp until just orange, being careful not to over-cook. Remove and set aside.

7. Replenish small amount of oil if needed. Stir-fry tofu 2 minutes. Remove and set aside.

8. In a bowl, combine arrowroot powder, fish sauce, honey, cumin, marjoram, and lemon zest. In wok, heat and stir until simmering and slightly thickened. Add tamarind juice, bean sauce, pickled garlic, tofu, egg substitute-garlic-onion mix, and fried noodles. Gently mix until combined and heated.

9. Serve on fish platter topped with garnish.

Pomegranate-stuffed Eggplants

yield 2 servings

2 small Japanese or Italian eggplants (may substitute small zucchinis; reduce cooking time)

1/2 teaspoon salt

2 tablespoons olive oil

1 large yellow onion, chopped

1 cup fresh shiitake mushrooms, chopped

1 cup pomegranate, smashed (see Note, page 197)

2/3 tablespoons maple syrup

Pinch coarse sea salt

1/4 teaspoon black pepper, ground

1/4 teaspoon cumin

1/4 teaspoon cayenne pepper, crushed

1/8 teaspoon fresh basil, crushed

3 small sprigs saffron

1 tablespoon water

1/4 cup hazelnuts or cashews, toasted

1 tablespoon cooking sherry

1/2 tablespoon extra-virgin olive oil

1/3 red frying pepper or bell pepper, thinly sliced

1/4 cup water

3/4 tablespoon tomato paste

1/4 teaspoon fresh squeezed lemon juice

4 tablespoons fresh mint leaves for garnish

4 flat fresh leaf parsley sprigs for garnish

1 teaspoon succanat or raw sugar to taste

1. Remove stems from eggplants and discard. Gently roll each eggplant back and forth 4 or 5 times on counter to soften and facilitate removal of the insides. Using a spoon, tunnel through the eggplant to within a quarter inch of each end. Scoop out and discard pulp, leaving a thin shell approximately 1/8 inch in diameter.

2. In large bowl, dissolve 1/2 teaspoon salt in water. Add the eggplant skins and let soak.

3. Warm 2 tablespoons olive oil in medium skillet. Add onion, cover, and cook 5 minutes or until onions are softened, not browned. Uncover, and cook approximately 10 more minutes on medium heat, stirring occasionally.

4. Slowly increase heat to high and add mushrooms. Cook 2½ minutes, stirring. Add pomegranate and maple syrup, pinch of coarse sea salt, black pepper, cumin, cayenne, basil, saffron, and 1 table-spoon water. Cook approximately 2 minutes or until all water has cooked down. Remove from heat and gently fold in hazelnuts. Season to taste with black pepper, sea salt, and cooking sherry. Set aside to cool.

5. With paper towels, pat dry eggplants. Pack each eggplant with stuffing using small spoon. Save extra stuffing.

6. In a separate skillet, heat extra-virgin olive oil. Working in batches, lightly brown stuffed eggplants on all sides.

7. In a 4-quart casserole, arrange the eggplants in 1 layer. Fill in gaps with extra filling to increase aesthetic quality of casserole. Tuck the pepper slices between the eggplants.

8. Drain excess fat from the skillet, and add ¼ cup water, tomato paste, lemon juice, black pepper, and sea salt to taste. Bring to a full boil, slowly adding pomegranate-maple syrup mixture. Pour sauce over the eggplants. Top with fresh mint leaves.

9. Cook over low heat until tender, 15-25 minutes. Let stand 3-10 minutes in casserole.

10. Remove eggplants to serving dish. Strain the pan juices and set aside. Sauce should be creamy. Adjust flavor to taste with salt, pepper, or lemon juice. Spoon over the eggplants. Garnish with fresh parsley, and sprinkle with raw sugar or succant to taste.

Note *Cut pomegranate into quarters, separate red seeds from yellow chaff, and purée with 1 tablespoon water.*

Chapter 6

DESSERTS

African American

Sweet Potato Pie

Brazilian

Coco Cream Delight

Cuban

Empanaditas

Flan de Calabaza

English

Truly Trifle

Golden Strawberry

Blueberry Crumble

Orange Lightness

French

Bananes Flambées

Carob Soufflé

German

German Chocolatey Cake

Bavarian Apple Strudel

Fruit Salad

Hungarian

Crispy Cherries

Toasted Egg Barley

Indonesian

Spiced Fruit Salad

Irish

Raspberry Custard

Italian

Angelica Rice Lady Fingers

Jamaican

Sweet Cassava Pudding

Island Banana Cake

Banana Dessert Tamale

Green Plantain Balls

Polish

Orange Glazed Apples

Spanish

Flan

Thai

Sticky Sweet Rice on Papaya

Turkish

Festive Rice Milk Pudding

Citrus Celebration

Sweet Potato Pie

yield 4-6 servings

4 tablespoons canola oil

1 cup firmly packed date sugar or maple syrup

1 1/2 cups boiled, mashed sweet potatoes (2 large or 3 medium)

1/2 cup applesauce

2 tablespoons egg substitute

1/3 cup soy or rice milk

1 tablespoon fresh lemon juice

1 tablespoon freshly grated lemon zest

1 teaspoon pure vanilla extract

1/2 teaspoon freshly grated nutmeg

1/4 teaspoon sea salt

1 prepared 9-inch whole-grain pie shell (spelt is ideal)

1.   Preheat oven to 425°.

2.   In a large bowl, blend oil and date sugar until light and fluffy. Mix in sweet potatoes and applesauce. Add egg substitute and beat vigorously.

3.   While adding rice milk, lemon juice, lemon zest, vanilla, nutmeg, and sea salt, continue beating mixture to a smooth, creamy consistency.

4.   Pour the mixture into the pie shell and bake for 10 minutes. Then lower the temperature to 325° and bake for an additional 35 minutes or until a knife inserted into the center of the pie comes out clean.

Coco Cream Delight

yield 2 servings

1 cup Nut Quick
1/2 teaspoon orange zest
1 can thick coconut milk
1/4 cup egg substitute
1/4 cup date sugar plus extra
  for garnish
1 tablespoon honey

1/8 cup cashews, chopped
1/2 cup fresh coconut,
  shredded
2 coconuts, split in two
1 teaspoon lemon juice
1 teaspoon lime juice
1 teaspoon rum

1. Preheat oven to 300°.

2. Purée Nut Quick, orange zest, coconut milk, egg substitute, 1/4 cup date sugar, and honey in blender. Stir in nuts and coconut. Pour into ovenproof dish and bake for 25 minutes or until a knife inserted in the center comes out clean.

3. Remove from oven, cool slightly, and then refrigerate 4-6 hours.

4. Spoon chilled custard mixture into coconut halves.

5. Combine lemon juice, lime juice, and rum. Drizzle over coconut halves. Sprinkle date sugar on top.

6. Carefully caramelize tops under the broiler. Watch constantly, since this will occur rapidly.

Empanaditas

yield 2 servings

DOUGH

1 cup spelt flour, plus extra
for coating

1/2 tablespoon salt

1/2 tablespoon honey

1 tablespoon olive oil

1/4 cup egg substitute

1/4-1/2 teaspoon allspice

2 tablespoons water

FILLING

2 Red Delicious apples,
thinly sliced

1/4 teaspoon cinnamon

Handful raisins or dried
cherries

Vegetable oil for frying

1.   *To prepare the dough:* Combine all ingredients together in a bowl and mix until smooth. Roll into 2-inch balls.

2.   *To prepare the filling:* In a bowl, combine apples, cinnamon, and raisins.

3.   Coat each ball with flour and hold it in your left hand. Use your right hand to flatten out a pocket in the dough ball.

4.   Stuff pocket with filling and close dough over it.

5.   Fry the empanaditas over high heat, four at a time, until golden. Drain on paper towels.

N o t e   *Besides fruit, filling can be fish or vegetables.*

Flan de Calabaza

yield 2 servings

Canola oil

3 tablespoons brown rice
   syrup

1/4 cup honey

1 cup cooked or canned
   pumpkin

1/4 cup rice milk

Pinch cinnamon

Pinch salt

2 tablespoons arrowroot

3 teaspoons vanilla extract

1 teaspoon almond extract

1. Preheat oven to 350°.

2. Oil a small baking dish, and spread brown rice syrup evenly on bottom.

3. In a small bowl, combine all other ingredients until smooth, then pour over brown rice syrup.

4. Bake for 45 minutes. Refrigerate. Serve chilled.

Truly Trifle

yield 2 servings

TRIFLE

1 honey cake (8 ounces) or pound cake

1/2 cup raspberry jam with seeds

2 tablespoons apricot brandy

2 tablespoons sherry

1/2 cup slivered almonds

3/4 cup rice milk

1/2 cup powdered goat milk, or rice or soy milk mixed with 1/4 cup iced water

1 tablespoon date sugar

1 tablespoon honey

1 tablespoon arrowroot powder

3/4 cup egg substitute

1/2 teaspoon pure vanilla extract

1/2 teaspoon pure almond extract

1/4 cup coconut milk

1/4 teaspoon cinnamon

1/4 teaspoon nutmeg

1 cup tofutti or tofu cream cheese, whipped

Lemon slices or crystallized nasturtiums for garnish

CASHEW NUT CREME

1/2 cup raw cashews

1 cup water, or 1 cup plain or vanilla soy milk for a thicker cream

3 dates, pitted, or 1 tablespoon honey

1/8 teaspoon pure vanilla extract

Pinch sea salt

1. *To prepare the trifle:* Select either a medium glass bowl or parfait glasses. Cut honey cake into thick slices and spread with raspberry jam. Pack slices tightly into bottom of container.

2. Mix brandy and sherry and pour over honey cake. Top with slivered almonds and set aside for 30 minutes, no longer.

3. In a double boiler, bring milks, date sugar, honey, and arrowroot to a boil, stirring constantly.

4. Whisk in egg substitute one tablespoon at a time and continue cooking and stirring until thick. Do not let the mixture boil.

5. Remove from heat and gently stir in vanilla and almond extracts, coconut milk, cinnamon, and nutmeg.

6. Let custard cool until barely warm, and then pour it over cake. Refrigerate. When trifle is completely cool, distribute remaining jam on top. Top with a dollop of tofutti or cashew nut creme. Decorate with lemon slice or crystallized nasturtiums.

7. *To prepare the cashew creme:* Blend cashews, water, dates, vanilla, and salt in a blender until very smooth, 2-3 minutes.

Golden Strawberry Blueberry Crumble

yield 2 servings

1/4 cup spelt flour

1/2 cup rice flour

1 tablespoon arrowroot

1 cup date sugar, divided

3 ounces canola margarine, melted

1 cup fresh or frozen blueberries

1 cup fresh or frozen strawberries

2 teaspoons freshly squeezed lemon juice

1/4 teaspoon cinnamon

1 tablespoon flaked coconut, fresh or packaged

1. Preheat oven to 300°.

2. In a large bowl, mix flours, arrowroot, and 3/4 cup date sugar. Add melted canola margarine with pastry blender until crumbles resemble bread crumb lumps.

3. Place blueberries and strawberries in a soufflé dish and sprinkle them with lemon juice, remaining 1/4 cup date sugar, and cinnamon.

4. Cover berries evenly with the crumble mixture. Press topping down gently.

5. Bake for 15-20 minutes, or until crumble is golden. Serve hot or cold, sprinkled with coconut.

Orange Lightness

yield 2 servings

1 envelope unflavored gelatin

2 tablespoons boiling water

2 tablespoons egg white powder; equivalent to 2 egg whites, reconstituted

1/4 teaspoon cream of tartar

1/4 cup egg substitute

1/3 cup date sugar

1 teaspoon honey (orange blossom is ideal)

Juice of one orange

1 tablespoon orange zest

1 teaspoon lemon juice

1 teaspoon lime juice

1 cup rice milk

1. Dissolve gelatin in 1 cup boiling water. Set aside to cool.

2. Combine reconstituted egg whites and cream of tartar. Beat until stiff peaks form. Refrigerate for 2 hours.

3. In the top of a double boiler over medium-low heat, mix egg substitute with date sugar and honey. Stir in orange juice, zest, and lemon and lime juices.

4. In a blender, whip rice milk on high speed to aerate. Mix in egg-sugar mixture.

5. In a soufflé dish, combine gelatin and rice milk mixture. Gently fold in chilled egg whites. Chill for 2 or more hours and serve.

Bananes Flambées

yield 2 servings

3 ripe but not discolored
  bananas

1¹/₂ tablespoons canola
  margarine

¹/₂ teaspoon butter

1 tablespoon date sugar

2 tablespoons honey, preferably orange blossom

Dash of ground cinnamon

¹/₄ cup orange juice
  concentrate

¹/₂ teaspoon orange zest

¹/₄ cup golden raisins

1 teaspoon vanilla extract

2 tablespoons dark rum

Fresh mint leaves for garnish

1.　Peel bananas, and slice in half lengthwise. Discard the peels.

2.　Heat canola margarine and butter in a nonstick frying pan
and add the bananas, placing the round side down first. Cook approximately 5 minutes on each side.

3.　Mix together the date sugar, honey, cinnamon, orange juice
concentrate, orange zest, raisins, and vanilla, and pour over the
bananas. Cook 10 minutes more.

4.　Just before serving, remove the banana halves and arrange
them on serving plates.

5.　Heat the juices so bubbles are beginning, add rum, and
ignite sauce. Pour over bananas with a flourish. Garnish with fresh
mint leaves.

Carob Soufflé

yield 2 servings

1/3 cup date sugar, plus extra for dusting	1/2 tablespoon macadamia or canola oil
1/8 cup soy flour	1 cup egg substitute
2/3 cup unflavored soy or rice milk, divided	1 1/2 teaspoons pure vanilla extract
1/2 cup carob powder	1 1/2 teaspoons baking powder

1. Preheat oven to 375°.

2. Oil a 1 quart soufflé dish and dust with date sugar, shaking off the excess. Fit the dish with an oiled and sugared parchment paper or foil collar extending 2 inches above the rim.

3. In a bowl, whisk together 1/4 cup date sugar, flour, and 2 1/2 tablespoons milk and set aside. Scald the remaining milk in a saucepan. Place in blender and blend at high speed with carob powder until there are no lumps

4. Transfer milk-carob mixture to the saucepan and heat on a low simmer, stirring, for 2 minutes. Remove from heat and whisk in macadamia oil.

5. Return mixture to blender and blend in egg substitute. Then blend in sugar-flour mixture. Add vanilla, remaining sugar, and remaining milk, and blend again. Finally, add baking powder and blend just until well mixed.

6. Immediately fold out into prepared soufflé dish.

7. Bake until puffed, about 35 minutes.

8. Serve warm with raspberries or cut strawberries.

German Chocolatey Cake

yield 4 servings

TOPPING
3/4 cup date sugar
1/3 cup coconut oil
3/4 cup soy milk powder
    mixed with 1/4 cup water
1/2 cup pecans, roughly
    chopped
1/3 cup fresh flaked or grated
    coconut

TO CONTINUE THE RECIPE
3 ounces carob chips (dark is
    ideal)
1 cup date sugar

1/2 cup canola margarine
1 cup egg substitute
1 teaspoon pure vanilla
    extract
1 teaspoon butter flavor
    extract
1/2 cup soy flour
1/2 cup spelt flour
3/4 teaspoon baking soda
Pinch sea salt
1/2 cup water
1 teaspoon white vinegar
1/4 cup soy milk

1. *To prepare the topping:* Preheat oven to 350°. Oil an 8-inch square baking pan and dust with flour.

2. In a heavy saucepan, combine date sugar, coconut oil, and reconstituted soy milk over medium-low heat for 10 minutes. Stir frequently.

3. Remove from heat, and add pecans and coconut. Distribute evenly over bottom of prepared pan. Set aside.

4. *To continue the recipe:* In the top of a double boiler over medium-high heat, melt carob chips, stirring until the chips are liquefied. Set aside.

5. In a large mixing bowl, cream date sugar and canola margarine until fluffy. Beat in egg substitute. Stir in melted carob and vanilla and butter extracts.

6. In a separate bowl, mix flours, baking soda, and salt.

7. In a small bowl, whisk together water and vinegar.

8. Combine flour mixture with soy milk. Add to the carob mixture and blend until smooth.

9. Pour over topping in cake pan, and bake until toothpick inserted in center of cake comes out clean, about 40 minutes. Do not overcook.

10. Remove from oven and cool on a wire rack for 10-5 minutes. Loosen cake by running a knife around the rim of the pan. Turn cake upside down over serving plate, and lift pan off. Cool completely before serving.

Note *Store in airtight container or wrapping to retain moistness.*

Bavarian Apple Strudel

yield 2 servings

1/4 cup organic raisins

1 tablespoon almond extract

1 teaspoon vanilla extract

1 1/4 pounds mixed Red Delicious and Granny Smith apples

1 1/2 cups cold water mixed with 1 tablespoon freshly squeezed lemon juice

1/3 cup plus 1 tablespoon date sugar

1 teaspoon orange zest

1/2 teaspoon cinnamon

1/2 cup soy flour

1/2 cup spelt flour

2 tablespoons hazelnut oil, divided

1/8 teaspoon sea salt

1/3 cup water

1 tablespoon walnut oil

1/2 cup hazelnuts, finely chopped

3/4 cup soy milk powder mixed with 1/2 cup water

1 tablespoon honey

1. Plump raisins by soaking them in the almond and vanilla extracts. Set aside.

2. Peel and core apples. Cut crosswise into thin slices. Cover with cold water and lemon juice. Set aside.

3. Combine 1/3 cup date sugar, orange zest, and cinnamon. Set aside.

4. Mix flours, 1 tablespoon hazelnut oil, salt, and 1/3 cup water until flour is moistened and dough cleans side of bowl.

5. Turn dough out on a lightly floured surface. Knead until smooth and no longer sticky. If the dough is too sticky, add flour; if it is too taut, add a few drops of water.

6. Preheat oven to 375°. Oil a cookie sheet.

7. Shape dough into a ball and brush with oil. Cover and let rest in a warm place for 30 minutes.

8. Drain apples, combine with sugar-orange mixture and chopped hazelnuts.

9. On a floured cloth, roll dough out into a $^1/_8$-inch thick square. Brush with remaining hazelnut oil and spread with apple mixture.

10. Roll up and bake 30-35 minutes.

11. Remove from oven. Mix soy milk and honey and drizzle over strudel. Serve warm.

Fruit Salad

yield 2 servings

1 orange

1 apple

1 banana

1/8 cup pecans or almonds, chopped

2 tablespoons date sugar or maple syrup

1 tablespoon freshly squeezed lemon juice

3 tablespoons shredded coconut

Fresh mint sprigs

1. Peel orange, apple, and banana. Dice fruit and mix together in large, chilled bowl.

2. Add nuts, sugar, lemon juice, and shredded coconut, and mix well.

3. Garnish with mint leaves and serve.

Crispy Cherries

y i e l d   2   s e r v i n g s

$^1/2$ cup date sugar

$^1/2$ cup soy flour

$^1/8$ teaspoon sea salt

$^1/4$ cup soy or rice milk

$^1/4$ cup vanilla extract

$^1/2$ cup egg substitute

Canola oil for frying

$^1/2$ pound fresh, ripe, hard
  pears or grapes

$^1/2$ teaspoon cinnamon

1.   Blend date sugar in a blender on high speed for 2 minutes.

2.   In a large bowl, mix flour, $^1/4$ cup date sugar, salt, milk, and vanilla to a smooth batter. Stir in the egg substitute.

3.   Heat 3 inches of oil in deep pan. Dip pears or grapes into the batter, making sure they are well coated. In small batches (so that oil temperature remains hot), quickly plunge fruit into hot oil. Remove with a skimmer as soon as they are browned, and drain on paper towels.

4.   Combine remaining $^1/4$ cup date sugar with cinnamon and sprinkle generously on fruit. Serve warm.

Hungarian

Toasted Egg Barley

yield 2 servings

1/2 cup egg barley
1 tablespoon walnut oil
1/4 teaspoon sea salt
1 teaspoon paprika
2 cups water

1 teaspoon fresh lemon juice

SAUCE

3 tablespoons orange juice
1 tablespoon honey
1/4 cup water

1.   Preheat oven to 350°.

2.   In a pan over medium heat, lightly brown egg barley in oil for 20 minutes. Add salt and paprika and stir to combine well.

3.   Cover barley with water and simmer until the water is absorbed, about 15 minutes.

4.   Transfer barley to ovenproof dish. Cover and bake until tender, about 45 minutes.

5.   *To prepare the sauce*: Combine all ingredients in a saucepan and heat until warm. Do not boil.

6.   Drizzle sauce over the baked egg barley and serve warm.

Spiced Fruit Salad

yield 2 servings

SAUCE

$^1/_2$ cup roasted almonds

$^1/_2$ cup honey

$^1/_8$ teaspoon cayenne

$^1/_2$ cup water

1$^1/_2$ teaspoon vanilla extract

FRUIT

1 cup jicama, thinly sliced

2 cups banana, cubed

1 cup pineapple, cubed

1 cup peeled apple, cored
and sliced

1 cup firm papaya, chopped

1. *To prepare the sauce:* In a blender or food processor, chop almonds, then blend in remaining sauce ingredients.

2. Arrange fruits on a platter and serve with sauce on the side.

Raspberry Custard

yield 2 servings

1 cup vanilla-flavored rice
  milk

1/8 cup honey

1/2 cup egg substitute

1/8 teaspoon salt

1 teaspoon fruit pectin

3/4 cup raspberry jam

Canola oil for oiling baking
  pan

1 package (14 ounces) Tree
  of Life Peach Apricot
  Cookies, or cookies of
  your choice

1/3 cup sherry mixed with
  1/3 cup ice water

10 ounces frozen raspberries

1 tablespoon dried coconut

3/4 cup soy powder or powdered goat's milk

1 cup water

1/4 cup date sugar

1 tablespoon rum

Raspberries for garnish

1. In saucepan over medium heat, scald milk and honey. Slowly
stir in egg substitute, salt, and pectin. Continue stirring while mixture bubbles for 2-3 minutes. Pour into a bowl and chill in freezer
while remaining ingredients are prepared.

2. Melt jam and set aside.

3. Oil a bread pan (preferably glass). Line bottom of pan with
one layer of cookies.

4. Drizzle half the diluted sherry over the cookies. Spread
cookies with half the melted jam. Sprinkle half the raspberries and
coconut on top of jam. Pour a ribbon of custard over this with half
the custard. Repeat the layering. Cover with plastic wrap and chill in
refrigerator 2-3 hours.

5. Beat soy powder and water together, and add date sugar and
rum. Spoon over chilled custard. Garnish with 3 raspberries on each
serving.

Angelica Rice Lady Fingers

yield 2 servings

2 cups light rice flour, plus extra for dusting

2 tablespoons buckwheat flour

2 tablespoons extra fine soy flour

3/4 teaspoon baking soda

1 tablespoon succanat

1/2 teaspoon sea salt

1 teaspoon vanilla extract

1/8 teaspoon almond extract

1/2 cup egg substitute

1/8 teaspoon lemon juice

6 tablespoons maple syrup

1.   Preheat oven to 375°.

2.   Sift together flours, baking soda, succanat, and sea salt.

3.   In separate bowl, beat together remaining ingredients until well blended.

4.   Combine dry and wet mixtures until a light, airy dough forms. Add a little flour or water to obtain right consistency.

5.   Dust cutting board with rice flour. Place dough ball in center and gently roll out dough with rice flour dusted rolling pin until approximately 1 1/2 inches thick. Do not overwork the dough. Using a cookie cutter or free style, cut cookies from the dough.

6.   Place on cookie sheet and bake for approximately 8-10 minutes, or until edges are slightly brown.

Sweet Cassava Pudding

yield 2 servings

1¹/2 cups sweet cassava flour

¹/4 cup whole wheat pastry flour

¹/4 teaspoon sea salt

³/4 cup date sugar or raw honey

¹/2 teaspoon lemon zest

¹/2 cup grated coconut

2 tablespoons macadamia oil

1¹/2 cups coconut cream

¹/2 cup egg substitute

¹/2 teaspoon almond extract

1. Preheat oven to 350°. Oil an 8-inch square glass or nonstick baking pan.

2. In a medium bowl, mix both flours, salt, date sugar, lemon zest, and coconut.

3. In separate bowl, blend remaining ingredients until smooth.

4. Combine dry and wet ingredients until smooth. Pour into baking pan and bake until pudding is set, 45-55 minutes.

5. Serve warm.

Island Banana Cake

yield 2 servings

1/4 cup honey
1/2 cup date sugar
1/4 cup walnut oil
2/3 cup mashed ripe bananas
1/4 cup egg substitute
1/3 cup rice or soy milk
1 teaspoon freshly squeezed
  lemon juice
1 cup spelt flour
1/4 teaspoon sea salt

1/4 cup honey crunch wheat
  germ
1 teaspoon baking powder
1/2 teaspoon baking soda
1/2 teaspoon cinnamon
1/8 teaspoon nutmeg
1/4 teaspoon anise seed
1/2 cup golden raisins or
  chopped apricots
1/4 cup hazelnuts, chopped

1. Preheat oven to 350°.

2. Blend together honey, sugar, and oil.

3. In a separate bowl, blend bananas, egg substitute, milk, and lemon juice. Combine with the honey mixture and blend until smooth.

4. Sift flour, salt, wheat germ, baking powder, baking soda, cinnamon, nutmeg, and anise into the wet ingredients. Fold in fruit and nuts.

5. Grease and flour a large pan. Pour in batter and bake for 45 minutes or until knife inserted into the center comes out clean.

Banana Dessert Tamale

yield 4 servings

4 green bananas, peeled and
grated

1/3 cup dry coconut flakes

1 cup whole wheat pastry
flour

1/4 cup wheat germ, plain or
honey crunch

1 cup date sugar or honey

2 tablespoons vanilla extract

1/2 tablespoon freshly ground
nutmeg

1 tablespoon almond extract

Pinch of sea salt

4 large banana leaves

1. Combine all ingredients, except banana leaves, into a smooth batter. Place a quarter of the mixture onto each banana leaf. Wrap each packet snugly and tie with string.

2. Bring a large pot of water to a boil. Add the packets to the water, cover, and cook for 1 hour.

3. Remove packets, unwrap them when cool enough to handle, and serve warm.

Green Plantain Balls

yield 2 servings

1 green plantain, left in its
   peel

4 teaspoons honey

2 teaspoons almond extract

2 teaspoons vanilla extract

Sea salt to taste

Callaloo or cooked spinach
   (optional)

Jamaican Run Down
   (optional; page 174)

Optional Topping (below)

1.   Place the plantain in a pot of unsalted water to cover and
bring to a boil. Add the honey and extracts, and boil until tender,
about 30 minutes. Remove and let cool.

2.   When cool enough to touch, remove and discard the peel.
Slice the flesh and season with sea salt.

3.   Serve warm with callaloo (or spinach, if callaloo isn't available), Jamaican Run Down, or the optional topping below.

Optional Topping   *Mix 2 tablespoons honey, 1/2 teaspoon rum, 1
teaspoon hot water, 4 tablespoons coconut milk, and flaked coconut
together in a small bowl. Pour over plantain.*

Orange Glazed Apples

yield 2 servings

2 large Red Delicious apples
1/4 cup maple syrup
2 tablespoons grated orange
    zest

1/4 cup orange juice
1/2 tablespoon canola oil
1/2 tablespoon ground
    cinnamon

1.   Core and quarter the apples and set aside.

2.   In a saucepan, combine the maple syrup, orange zest and juice, oil, and cinnamon. Simmer for 10 minutes.

3.   Add the apples to the glaze, making sure to cover them well. Cook in a covered saucepan for 10-15 minutes. Serve immediately.

Flan

yield 2 servings

1/4 cup maple syrup
1/8 cup water
1 teaspoon almond extract
1/2 tablespoon vanilla extract
3/4 cup rice or soy milk

1/4 cup cornstarch
1/3 cup soft or silken tofu
1/4 cup pecan pieces, chopped

1. In a small nonstick saucepan, combine the syrup and water. Bring to a boil, then lower heat to a simmer, making sure to swirl the pan while mixture thickens and caramelizes.

2. Pour enough of the mixture into the flan mold to cover the bottom.

3. Preheat oven to 350°.

4. Combine almond and vanilla extracts, milk, cornstarch, tofu, and pecans, and blend until smooth. Pour into a mold, and cover with foil.

5. Place mold in a pan. Fill pan with water to within an inch of the top of the mold.

6. Bake 40-50 minutes. Allow flan to cool completely before removing from mold. Serve warm.

Sticky Sweet Rice on Papaya

yield 2 servings

2¹/4 cups coconut milk

¹/3 cup honey

¹/4 teaspoon sea salt

1 cup basmati short grain white rice, rinsed

2 ripe, seeded papaya, cut in half

1 teaspoon fresh lemon juice

1 teaspoon sunflower seeds

Thick coconut cream (optional topping)

4 mint leaves for garnish

1. Bring coconut milk and honey to a boil in a large saucepan, then add salt and cook for 5 minutes. Add rice, stir, and reduce heat to simmer. Cover, and check after 20 minutes. Remove from heat when all liquid has been absorbed.

2. Sprinkle each papaya half with lemon juice and sunflower seeds. Top with rice mixture. Add a dollop of coconut cream (if desired), and garnish with one mint leaf.

Festive Rice Milk Pudding

yield 2 servings

1/2 cup egg substitute

1 tablespoon arrowroot
   powder

1 tablespoon rice flour

1/3 cup water or fruit juice

2 cups plain or vanilla rice
   milk

1/3 cup honey

1/8 cup cashews, ground

1/8 cup dried, flaked coconut

1/4 cup dried cherries

1/4 cup dried apricots

Pinch of sea salt

1/2 teaspoon pure almond
   extract

4 tablespoons raw honey

Freshly ground cinnamon for
   garnish

1.　Mix well egg substitute, arrowroot powder, rice flour, and 1/3 cup water or fruit juice.

2.　Whisk in milk and honey, then transfer mixture to a deep saucepan. Bring to a boil, stirring constantly. Reduce heat to low.

3.　Add cashews, coconut, cherries, apricots, and salt. Simmer and stir for 18 minutes or until thickened, then add almond extract.

4.　Pour the pudding into 2 individual ovenproof crocks, drizzle with honey, and brown lightly under the broiler.

5.　Serve immediately sprinkled with freshly ground cinnamon, or cover and chill for several hours.

Citrus Celebration

yield 2 servings

3 tablespoons arrowroot powder

1/4 cup freshly squeezed lemon juice

1 1/2 cup fresh grapefruit juice

1 teaspoon lemon zest

2 teaspoons honey (preferably orange blossom)

1 pink or red grapefruit, peeled and sectioned

1 orange, peeled and sectioned

1/2 cup Nut Quick (available in health food stores)

1/4 cup toasted coconut flakes

1/4 cup pistachio nuts, chopped

1. Whisk together arrowroot powder, lemon and grapefruit juices, lemon zest, and honey in a saucepan. Bring to a boil while stirring constantly. Reduce heat, simmer, and continue stirring for 5 minutes.

2. Gently fold in grapefruit and orange sections. Simmer for 2 more minutes.

3. Fold in Nut Quick and coconut, and cook 5 minutes longer.

4. Pour into separate dessert cups or one large bowl.

5. Serve chilled, garnished with chopped pistachio nuts.

Chapter 7

DRESSINGS, SAUCES, AND SPREADS

Chinese

Date Paste

Ginger Black Bean Pâté

English

Mint Sauce

Horseradish Sauce

Indonesian

Hot Peanut Dipping Sauce

Jamaican

Tropical Vinaigrette

Mexican

Anytime Salsa

Turkish

Healthy Lemon-Egg Sauce

Lively Lemon-Lime Sauce

Date Paste

1 cup cooked red kidney
  beans

1/2 cup ground cashews

3 tablespoons crystallized
  honey

2 teaspoons dates, finely
  chopped

1/4 teaspoon sea salt

1 teaspoon dried mint

1 teaspoon almond extract

1 teaspoon vanilla extract

1.   Rub beans through a food mill or a wire sieve to make a paste.

2.   Add all other ingredients to bean paste and stir to combine thoroughly. Refrigerate. Use on crackers or as dip for vegetables.

Ginger Black Bean Pâté

yield 2 servings

1 cup cooked black beans
1 tablespoon tamari
1/2 teaspoon chili paste
1 tablespoon spelt flour

2 tablespoons sesame oil, divided
2 cloves garlic, minced
1 teaspoon minced ginger
1/4 teaspoon sea salt

1. Mash beans with a ricer or potato masher.

2. Add tamari and chili paste, and stir to combine well.

3. Stir in flour and 1/2 tablespoon oil, and mix well.

4. In a pan, heat the remaining 1 1/2 tablespoons sesame oil, and sauté garlic, ginger, and salt. Cook, stirring constantly, for 2 minutes.

5. Add garlic-ginger mixture to beans, stirring to combine thoroughly.

6. Refrigerate but do not freeze. Use on bread and crackers or with vegetables.

Mint Sauce

yield 2 servings

1 cup fresh mint or
  spearmint, no stems, finely
  chopped
$^1/_4$ cup water

1 teaspoon white powdered
  stevia (available in health
  food stores), or $^1/_2$ cup
  raw sugar
$^1/_3$ cup red wine vinegar

1. Boil mint in water for 5 minutes. Remove from heat and let steep, covered, for 15 minutes.

2. Add the stevia powder and vinegar. Stir and serve with new baby potatoes.

Horseradish Sauce

yield 2 servings

$1/4$ cup freshly grated horse-radish

1 teaspoon Bragg's apple cider vinegar

1 teaspoon rice vinegar

1 teaspoon dry white wine

$1/8$ teaspoon white powdered stevia, or $3/4$ teaspoon raw sugar

$1/4$ teaspoon ground mustard

Pinch sea salt

Pinch garlic powder

$1/4$ teaspoon curry powder

$1/3$ cup powdered soy milk mixed with 2 tablespoons water

1. In a small bowl, mix horseradish, both vinegars, wine, stevia, mustard, sea salt, garlic, and curry powder.

2. Fold the reconstituted soy milk into the other ingredients. Chill several hours. Serve with broiled fish or a mild tofu dish.

Hot Peanut Dipping Sauce

yield 2 servings

1 hot red chile pepper,
  seeded and diced, or
  $^1/_8$ teaspoon cayenne
$^1/_8$ cup lemon juice
$^1/_8$ cup lime juice

4 whole scallions, diced
2 teaspoons honey
1 teaspoon sea salt
$^1/_2$ cup smooth peanut butter

1. In a blender or food processor, blend the chile, lemon and lime juices, scallions, honey, and salt to form a paste.

2. Add to the paste the peanut butter, blending. Add hot water as needed to make a thick sauce. Serve warm with vegetables for dipping.

Tropical Vinaigrette

yield 2 servings

3/4 cup extra-virgin olive oil

1/4 cup fresh lime juice

2 tablespoons fresh chives, chopped

1 shallot, minced

2 cloves garlic, crushed

1 tablespoon fresh parsley, chopped

1 tablespoon capers

1 teaspoon thyme, chopped

1/2 Scotch Bonnet chile, seeded and minced

1/2 teaspoon sea salt

1 tablespoon fresh lemon juice

2-3 tablespoons boiling water

1. Put all ingredients, except boiling water, into a blender. Blend at medium speed.

2. Add boiling water, one tablespoon at a time, to taste. Allow to stand 1 hour. Shake before using.

Note *This will keep up to one week in the refrigerator.*

Anytime Salsa

yield 2 servings

2 tablespoons white onion, diced

1 dash cayenne

1 teaspoon sea salt

1/2 teaspoon succanat

1 teaspoon red bell peppers, finely chopped

1 teaspoon green bell peppers, finely chopped

1 tablespoon freshly squeezed lime juice

8 Roma tomatoes, diced

2 serrano chiles, with seeds, finely diced

2 tablespoons cilantro leaves, finely chopped

1.   Place onion in a colander, and run hot water over it for 1-2 minutes.

2.   Place all ingredients in a bowl and mix well. Add more succanat if salsa is too acidic.

Healthy Lemon-Egg Sauce

yield 2 servings

3 tablespoons egg substitute

1 teaspoon arrowroot or cornstarch

$1/2$ cup vegetable broth (vegetable bouillon plus water)

4 tablespoons fresh lemon juice, strained

$1/2$ teaspoon Jane's Krazy Mixed-up Salt or sea salt

$1/2$ teaspoon lemon zest

1. In a saucepan, whisk egg substitute with arrowroot, and a small amount of vegetable broth, until mixture is smooth and shiny.

2. Add remaining broth, lemon juice, salt, and zest.

3. Cook over medium-low heat, whisking continuously until sauce reaches desired thickness. Never permit sauce to boil.

4. Serve over fish, steamed vegetables, or potatoes.

Lively Lemon-Lime Sauce

yield 2 servings

3 tablespoons avocado oil

3 tablespoons freshly
squeezed lemon juice

3 tablespoons freshly
squeezed lime juice

$^1/_3$ cup fresh mint, minced

1 tablespoon fresh cilantro

$^1/_2$ teaspoon Jane's Krazy
Mixed-up Salt

1. In a bowl, whisk all ingredients together. Refrigerate promptly.

2. Serve chilled on salad or fish.

Index

Stew
    almost locrio, 167
    black bean, 106–7
    mock meatball veggie, 153
    spring, 37
    tuna, eggplant, and chick pea, 104
    vegetable, 24

Stock, fish 'n chick pea peppercorn, 38

Strawberry blueberry crumble, 206

Strudel, apple, Bavarian, 212–13

Stuffed Grape Leaves, 75

Stuffed Head of Cabbage, 145

Sturgeon, tamarindo jerked, 170

Sweet Cassava Pudding, 220

Sweet Potato Pie, 200

Swordfish
    Enchilado, 128
    lemon, 117
    paprika, 143
    roast, marinated, 136–37
    and vegetable purée, soup, 12–13

Tahini, and garlic, eggplant, 76–77

Tamale, banana dessert, 222

Tamarindo Jerked Sturgeon, 170

Tempeh
    and bean sprouts, lo mein with, 118–19
    Cacciatora Sauce, 166
    rice with, 186
    sauce, white, linguine with, 155
    in Sherry Sauce, 188
    sweet and sour, 120

Thai dishes, 51, 52, 66, 94, 189–94, 226

Thai-style Salad, 66

Toasted Egg Barley, 216

Tofu
    with Broccoli, 122–23
    cucumber and, chilly, 67
    fish, and "no-meatballs," Spanish rice with, 184–85

goulash, 135
sliced, with garlic sauce, 126

Tomato(es)
    mushroom stuffed, 87
    red, pilaf, 83
    salad, herbed, 64

Tropical Vinaigrette, 235

Trout, cucumber, 152

Truly Trifle, 204–5

Tuna
    -Egg Balls, 71
    Eggplant, and Chick Pea Stew, 104
    and String Bean Ragout, 103

Turkish dishes, 53, 67, 95, 96, 196, 227, 228, 237, 238

Turned Down Cornmeal, 175

Vatapa, 112–13

Vegetable(-s, -ian)
    Chili, 178
    fish, and noodles, Dijon, 149–50
    fried, Japanese, 6
    Lasagna, 164–65
    Medley, 105
    mock meatball and, stew, 153
    purée and swordfish soup, 12–13
    rice and bean, soup, 40–41
    Root Soup, 46
    sautéed, with noodles, 132
    Stew, 24

Veracruz-style Red Snapper, 179

Vietnamese dish, 9

Vinaigrette
    roasted peppers with, 91
    tropical, 235

Welsh dish, 54

Yellow Bean Eggplant, 94

Yellow Rice, 86

Yucca, fried, 8

Ziti, baked, with portabello, 162–63